SUSANNA WESLEY
Mother of John and Charles

Susanna, the twenty-fifth child in her family, prayed daily, "Dear God, guide me. Make my life count." But God's answer seemed to be: *Wait.* So Susanna waited. And in the meantime, she married the young poet, Samuel Wesley.

Life with Samuel took Susanna from her life-long home in London to a new home over a hundred miles to the north. Samuel was a minister, but life in the rectory was not easy. There was never enough money to feed and clothe the family properly. Twice their house burned. One king after another reigned on the throne of England. And Samuel spent years writing his commentary on the Book of Job.

Through it all, Susanna devoted herself to her children—nineteen were born, but only nine lived to grow up. Would little Samuel ever learn to talk? How could she make time to spend alone with each of her children? When should she teach the children to read? And would her life ever count for something?

As a young woman, Susanna once said, "I hope the fire I start will not only burn all of London, but all of the United Kingdom as well. I hope it will burn all over the world."

ABOUT THE AUTHOR

When Charles Ludwig, author of over forty books, does his research for a new biography, he likes to see the places where the person he's writing about lived and traveled. Before he wrote *Susanna Wesley*, he spent a month in England visiting London, Epworth, Wroot, and other locations mentioned in this book. Some of the buildings that Susanna saw, and even one of the homes she lived in, are still standing today. Dr. Ludwig was able to photograph them, as well as areas where Susanna walked and traveled.

Dr. Ludwig lives in Arizona with his wife. They have a grown-up son and daughter who are both teachers. Even while Dr. Ludwig is writing one book, he is planning the next books he will write.

ABOUT THE ARTIST

Tim Bowers enjoys drawing humorous sketches as well as historical artwork. He lives in the town of Shawnee Mission, Kansas.

Mr. Bowers says, "I began drawing at a very early age. People and animals were my favorite subjects."

Susanna Wesley

Mother of John and Charles

by

Charles Ludwig

Illustrated by Tim Bowers

MOTT MEDIA

Milford, Michigan 48042

COPYRIGHT © 1984 by Mott Media, Inc.

Louise H. Rock, Editor
A. G. Smith, Cover Artist

LIBRARY OF CONGRESS CATALOGING IN PUBLICATION DATA

Ludwig, Charles
    Susanna Wesley: Mother of John and Charles.

    (The Sowers)
    Bibliography: p. 187
    Includes index.

    SUMMARY: A biography of the woman who married the well-known preacher, Samuel Wesley, and was the mother of John, founder of Methodism, and Charles, famous for the more than 6,000 hymns he wrote during his lifetime.
    1. Wesley, Susanna Annesley, 1669-1742—Juvenile literature. 2. Methodists—England—Biography—Juvenile literature. [1. Wesley, Susanna Annesley, 1669-1742. 2. Methodists] I. Bowers, Tim, ill. II. Title.
BX8495.W55L73 1984   287'.092'4   [B] [92] 84-60314
ISBN 0-88062-110-9 Paperbound
ISBN 0-88062-111-7 Hardcover

CONTENTS

ACKNOWLEDGMENTS

In addition to the librarians at Drew University; Duke University; Lovely Lane Museum in Baltimore; Asbury Theological Seminary; United Methodist Archives Center in Delaware, Ohio; Iliff School of Theology; McKendree College; and a few others where we visited, including the British Museum, we want to thank the following people who helped us with Methodist history:

Arthur Bruce Moss, Frank Baker, Edwin Schell, Asbury Smith, Kenneth E. Rowe, Herbert Huck, Jr., and several others. Likewise, I must thank the editor, Louise H. Rock, who pointed out several chronological errors, and suggested valuable improvements.

None of the above are to be blamed for my mistakes!

Leland D. Case, former editor of the *Rotarian*, and founder/editor of *Together*, also deserves special mention. Not only did he read the manuscript, but he lent books, and offered much helpful criticism. Having visited most Methodist places of special interest in both England and America in order to assemble material for *Together*, he is an extremely knowledgeable man.

Finally, we must express our thanks to Richard G. Kendall and his lovely wife, wardens of the Old Rectory in Epworth. They both overflow with knowledge, and they made our stay in Epworth one that we can never forget.

Susanna's World

Although she was Samuel Annesley's twenty-fifth and youngest child, Susanna feared her decision would hurt her father.

Pausing on the stairs that led up to her father's study in their Spital Square home, she reviewed the steps that had led to her decision. Placing the facts side by side like books on a shelf, she squinted at them. Yes, she was right! Long ago she had decided that she would make her life count! Still, she didn't want to hurt her father.

She glanced at the grandfather clock—it was ten till nine. This meant that her methodical parent had not quite finished the twenty chapters of the Bible which, from the time of his call to the ministry in his youth, he had promised to read each day of his life. Convinced she had better wait for a full ten minutes, Susanna attempted to calm herself by looking in the full-length mirror hanging on the newly papered wall.

She noted her features in the glass. Yes, she had to admit, she was reasonably attractive. Like the other

Annesleys, she was slim and just a little over five feet
tall. Her thin nose was triangular, well-formed, attractive; and although somewhat straight, her eyebrows
were heavy, dark, definite; and her no-nonsense chin
neither protruded nor receded.

After what seemed an eternity, the ten minutes
ticked by. Heart thumping, she climbed the carpeted
steps and gently tapped on the door marked with a
heavy sign: *Doctor Samuel Annesley, LL.D.*

"And what can I do for you?" asked Dr. Annesley,
lifting his eyes from an unrolled map on his large
wooden desk.

Susanna nervously shifted her feet on the carpet.
Both windows were wide open, and even though the
brisk January wind was tossing the curtains, her father
was coatless. "Sir, after much reading and a lot of
prayer, I have come to some definite conclusions—
conclusions which you may not like."

"About?"

"About the church, sir."

Frowning slightly, Annesley leaned back in his high-
backed chair and studied his daughter with playful,
and yet understanding eyes. Her abruptness amused
him. Thoughtfully he rubbed the end of his slightly
hooked, beak-like nose. "I know you've been studying a lot of history," he said. "You seem to have a
special interest in Oliver Cromwell. For a girl you do
a lot of reading!" He rolled the map and then unrolled
it again. "Tell me, Sukey, how old are you?"

"On January 20 I'll be thirteen."

"Thirteen? It seems hardly possible!" He rubbed
his chin, then made some calculations with his quill
pen. "Yes, I remember now. You were born on a
Wednesday, 1669. Outside our house the square was
white with snow. That was a remarkable year. That
was the same year Stradivari created his famous violin;

and it was also the year the great Rembrandt died,
and the year the guards in the Tower of London were
dubbed 'Beefeaters.' "

He picked up the map and tapped the end on his
desk. Then he leaned forward and said, "You have
a great mind, Sukey. Mother and I were talking about
it yesterday. We're proud of you."

"Yes, sir." Susanna bit her lip, and although her
heart was racing, she returned to her main stream of
thought. "As I was studying Cromwell and the
Dissenters—" A gust of wind lifted the map, dropped
it on the floor, and pushed it under the desk. Quickly
Susanna retrieved it and handed it to her father.
"Maybe I'd better close the windows," she suggested.
"It's terribly cold in here."

"Don't do that! Fresh air is good for the health.
Brightens the mind. Clears the lungs." From a top
drawer he withdrew a slender black stone about six
inches long. "Friend gave it to me. He said it was
from Asia Minor. It's a strange stone, and it does
strange things. But right now its job is to hold this
map down."

"As I was saying, sir—" Susanna was conscious
of trying to keep a tremor out of her voice. "I've been
thinking about the Dissenters; and, pardon me, sir,
I don't like some of the things they've done!"

"Such as?"

"Beheading King Charles, tearing up the *Book of
Common Prayer*, smashing crucifixes, burning
vestments, mocking the Church of England, break-
ing stained-glass windows in cathedrals, feeding their
horses in the churches, desecrating the high altars,
writing terrible books—"

Annesley raised his hand. "You're quite a girl!"
he exclaimed. "You're as independent as a cat! And
you're clever, proud, determined, and a little

stubborn. But you think for yourself, and I'm proud of you. Of course part of your trouble is that you are in the process of becoming a woman. You're in a difficult period of life. But don't worry. God will help you and you'll survive." He rubbed his chin.

"I hate to embarrass you, sir." Susanna said. "You are a very kind father, and I know you are the most famous dissenting preacher in all of London. A friend of mine said that you are the St. Paul of Dissenters. But I've made up my mind. Next Sunday I'm going to join the Church of England and start using the *Book of Common Prayer!*"

"You are going to join the Church of England?" Annesley repeated the words slowly, accenting each syllable. Then he retreated into a deep silence. As Susanna watched, his eyes became shiny and tears oozed from their edges. He started to speak, and then was silent. And as Susanna waited, a lump formed in her throat. She wondered why she'd been so cruel. Had it been possible, she would have disappeared.

Finally, her father cleared his throat, wiped his eyes, smiled, and said, "Sukey, go downstairs and bring me a piece of string, at least a yard long."

Mystified, for she knew she had hurt him deeply, Susanna almost ran down the steps. After rummaging under the bed, she found a ball of twine.

"I hope this is what you want," she said.

Without answering, Annesley tied one end around the middle of the flat stone and held it up so that it was suspended in the air. As the bar-like object moved in a circle, he said, "Now watch." In a few seconds it stopped moving.

"Which direction is it pointing?" he asked.

"North and south."

"Now you twist it."

Susanna wound the stone thirteen times before releasing it. This time it whirled for a full minute.

When it finally stopped, her father asked, "Which way is it pointing now?"

"North and south."

The preacher repeated the experiment a dozen times in various parts of his study; and on each occasion the bar stopped in a north and south position.

"Now get me a piece of straw, a needle, and a small pan of water."

Susanna studied him curiously. Was he feeling well? Convinced he was serious, she replied, "Yes, sir," and hurried down the steps.

When the items were on the desk, Susanna watched her father rub the needle on the black bar and then thrust it inside a fat piece of straw about its own length. He then gently placed the straw-enveloped needle lengthwise on the water in an east-west position. The moment he let go of it, the needle swung to a north-south position.

"What have I created?" he demanded. There was a note of triumph in his voice.

Susanna bit her lip. "A compass?" she answered after a long hesitation.

"That's right. We've made a compass. No, it's not as good as the one Columbus used in 1492. But it works on exactly the same principle that his worked on. Now I've done this to teach you a little theology." He poured the water into a plant and sat down.

"This black bar is a lodestone. The first lodestone was discovered in Magnesia—a country in Asia Minor. According to legend, it was discovered by a shepherd many years before the birth of Christ. This man discovered it when he noticed that it attracted the metal end of his staff.

"Centuries later, it was learned that a piece of steel could be given this mysterious pulling power by merely placing it on the lodestone; and because the lodestone was found in Magnesia, a piece of steel that was given its power is called a *magnet*.

"Hundreds of years after that discovery was common knowledge, the Chinese learned that if a tiny sliver of a lodestone was placed on a sliver of wood or in a bit of straw and floated on water, it would point to the north and south.

"The Arabs learned the secret from the Chinese; and the Europeans learned it from the Crusaders who had learned it from the Arabs. In this way it took over a thousand years for a ship-guiding compass to be invented. Now if it took that long to figure out such a simple thing as a compass, think how long it will take human beings to discover, I mean rediscover, the truths of the New Testament! For example, open the Bible and read the last part of Romans 1:17."

In a clear voice, Susanna read, "*The just shall live by faith.*"

"That's very simple. It's as simple as one plus one equals two. It means that we are saved through faith in God's grace. That truth was brought to the attention of the world by Martin Luther. But how long did it take for Luther to understand it?"

"I don't know."

"It took years. And Luther was a brilliant student of theology! He loved to read the Apostle Paul in his Bible. And he loved Paul's Book of Romans. Still, the truth didn't sink into Luther's heart until he was teaching the Book of Romans at Wittenberg in 1515." Annesley got up and began to pace back and forth.

"Did the people accept this truth right away?" he continued. "A few did. But many did not. Indeed, Luther had to go into hiding to keep from being killed. I, myself, was almost put to death because of what I believe."

He began to sniff the air. "I smell food. Maybe we'd better go downstairs."

At the foot of the steps, Annesley stopped. Then he placed a hand on each of Susanna's shoulders. "Do you know why we named you Susanna?" he asked.

"I have no idea."

"We named you after the Susanna in the Bible. She was one of the rich women who helped support Jesus and the twelve disciples. You can read about her in Luke 8:3."

"But I'm not rich!"

"No, you are not rich in money. But you are rich in character, determination, and intellect. And that, Sukey, is what counts!"

"Hurry!" cried a voice from the living room. "The food is getting cold!"

While Susanna was cutting a triangle of beef,

Annesley lifted his hand. "London is the largest city
in the world," he said. "From a third to half a million
souls live here. On Friday I'll take the day off and
visit my old church—St. Giles—and some other
historic places. All who want to go, raise your right
hand."

The only hand raised was that of Susanna.

"How about you, Elizabeth?" asked Annesley.

"Sorry," she answered. "But I'll be with John
Dunton at his print shop."

"Mmmm. Sounds as if a romance is developing!"
teased Annesley. Then, as Elizabeth blushed scarlet,
he faced Susanna. While massaging his chin, he said,
"You've been weighing the merits of the Dissenters.
On this trip I'll show you some points of high drama:
places where Dissenters were branded, had their ears
cut off, were made to stand with their heads and arms
in the pillory, and were burned alive."

Annesley continued eating in silence, and then he
looked at Susanna again. "Since I want you to get
as much out of this trip as possible," he said, "I want
you to make me a chart."

"A chart?" Susanna's eyes widened.

"Yes, a chart! Only a page or two. Start with Henry
VIII and diagram our rulers right through Cromwell
and up to our present king, Charles II."

Susanna frowned. "Do you want me to include all
five of Henry's wives?"

"Henry had six wives—"

"He had six, sir, if we count Anne of Cleves. But
Anne was so ugly he never lived with her. Indeed,
he was so angry with Thomas Cromwell for arrang-
ing the marriage, he ordered his head chopped off!"

Dr. Annesley smiled. "You're quite right, Sukey;
but do a good job. Such a chart can be quite useful."

GENEALOGY OF HENRY VIII AND JAMES II

All Henrys are Tudors; James and Charles are Stuarts

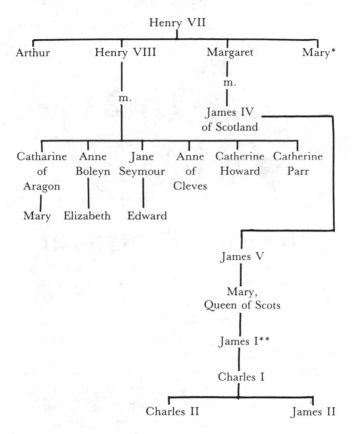

m. = married
* The line of Mary Tudor has not been traced.
** James I of England was also James VI of Scotland.

An easy way to remember the sequence and fate of
Henry's wives are the lines:

> Divorced, beheaded, died;
> Divorced, beheaded, survived!

Drama of Dissent

As Susanna slid next to her father in the coach, she felt a warm flush of pride. It was a privilege to be alone with him and to know that she would be reviewing some of the great dramas of history through his keen eyes. As the coach bumped and swayed, she handed him the chart.

Dr. Annesley was silent as he concentrated on the sheet of paper. Finally, after the carriage had sloshed through a section of mud, he said, "Sukey, you did a good job; and I'm glad you showed that Henry had six wives! But I'm worried about one thing."

"Yes?" She studied his face anxiously.

"Many in our time are confusing Christianity with politics. Some think that being a Protestant or a Catholic or a Dissenter is like belonging to a political party. Don't let this happen to you. *Real* Christianity is as certain as up or down."

The coach continued on to an area filled with

crowded, vile-smelling tenements, crisscrossed by narrow, twisting streets.

As Susanna watched, a woman emptied a slop-bucket out of a third-story window. Arcing down, the contents narrowly missed a man walking by. The woman was aiming for the sewer ditch running down the center of the street. Mercifully, it was almost bare. Susanna pinched her nose to shut out the odor.

"We're fortunate in being able to make this trip," said Dr. Annesley. "The only reason we can do so is because of the *Declaration of Indulgence* passed in 1672. Otherwise, I might be stopped and sentenced to the Tower of London!"

Susanna frowned. "Declaration of Indulgence? Please explain." Before he could answer, she added, "And, sir, please indulge me by closing the window. My t-teeth are ch-ch-chattering."

"Nonsense! Cold air is good for one. Men my age have to wear glasses. But I can read fine print without them. Why? Because I keep my windows open and drink only water. Besides we're almost there."

As Susanna stepped from the coach her father led her by the hand to a comfortable bench by the side of the massive building. "St. Giles goes back to almost the time of William the Conqueror in the eleventh century," he said, nodding toward the church. Its squarish steeple had four sets of windows on each side. The cemetery bristled with stone slabs standing on end.

"You've asked about the Declaration of Indulgence of 1672. To understand that we must know something about Henry VIII and his three children: Mary, Edward, and Elizabeth. Hand me the chart."

Pointing to the line which listed Henry's brother and sisters, he said, "Arthur, Henry's oldest brother, died in 1502. Being the oldest, Arthur was the Prince

of Wales, and had he lived, he would have become
King Arthur II! His death meant that Henry, born
in 1491, was the new heir. But there were complica-
tions. Four months before his death, Arthur had married Catherine of Aragon, daughter of Queen
Isabella—''

''The one who financed Columbus?'' Susanna
interrupted.

''Correct. It was then arranged for Henry to marry
Catherine.''

''But Catherine was his brother's widow!'' protested Susanna.

''That's the way it was done. One reason for this
move was to avoid offending Spain. Henry was only
twelve. Catherine was seventeen. But the ceremony
could not be performed until permission was received
from the Pope; and the Pope didn't even bother to
answer the request for three years. By the time permission was received, Henry was fifteen. Three years
later, Henry's father, Henry VII, died. Eighteen-year-
old Henry then followed him as Henry VIII. Henry
was a large man. I've seen his armor. He had massive
shoulders and was over six feet tall. With hair and
beard the color of fire, he was stunningly handsome.
But eighteen years after his marriage, he decided to
divorce Catherine.

''Facing her, he said, 'Catherine, since you were
married to my brother, we're living in sin! And that
may be the reason you don't have a son.'

''The real truth, Sukey, is that Henry had fallen
in love with Anne Boleyn—the black-eyed sister of
one of his mistresses! The Pope refused to grant him
a divorce. But that didn't stop Henry! He immediately
got two bills passed through Parliament in 1534. The
first severed the power of the Pope over England, and
the second made Henry the head of the Church of

England. That bill was called the *Act of Supremacy*."

"Did Henry VIII become a Protestant?"

"Politically, yes. Spiritually, no."

"Had he ever been converted?"

Dr. Annesley laughed. "Certainly not. To him, Christianity was merely a form. Like the majority of the upper classes in his age, he lived in open sin. But, in the depths of his heart, he remained Roman Catholic. You see, in his late twenties, Henry had written a book entitled *The Defense of the Seven Sacraments*. The purpose of this book was to denounce Luther's book, the *Babylonish Captivity*. Henry's book became very popular. It went into many translations and was reprinted twenty times. This book so pleased the Pope, he gave him the title, *Defender of the Faith*. Our kings and queens have been using that title ever since.

"Now that Henry was the head of the Church of England, he secured his divorce, and married Anne Boleyn. In time, Anne presented him with a daughter, Elizabeth. But three years after his marriage, Henry tired of Anne, and had her executed.

"Fearing the normal ax, Anne requested that an expert swordsman from Calais be employed. This man used a sword. Less than two weeks later, Henry married Jane Seymour. Jane presented him with his only son, Edward. Then she died.

"Since none of Henry's later wives had children, we'll forget them, and consider what happened to the offspring of his first three wives. But first, let's consider how Henry persecuted Protestants. In 1539 he pushed the *Act of Six Articles* through Parliament. Those six articles demanded that believers confess their sins to a priest; that only the priest was allowed to drink the wine in a communion service; that priests remain

single; and that everyone must believe in tran-
substantiation—that is the belief that when the communion bread and wine are blessed by the priest they
become the actual blood and body of Christ.''

Susanna bit her lip. ''And what was done to those
who didn't accept the *Six Articles*?''

''They lost their property. Many were even burned
at the stake. One man was hanged simply because he
ate meat during Lent!'' ·

''Sir, I'm in a shadow. It's cold. Let's move.''

Dr. Annesley was like a tightly wound watch. The
moment they were relocated in a patch of sun, he continued. ''Henry died in 1547. He was succeeded by
his son, Edward, who was crowned as Edward VI.
At the time, Edward was only ten years old.''

''But why wasn't Catherine's daughter, Mary,
made queen. She *was* the oldest!''

''Because the oldest male in a royal family is always
the heir. But back to the story. Edward VI was a true
Protestant, both politically and spiritually. And the
moment he came to power he released many Protestants imprisoned by his father.''

Annesley stood and stretched. Then he led Susanna
to the coach.

''I thought you were going to take me through St.
Giles!'' she protested.

''I am. But you'll understand the rest of the story
better if I take you to the actual place where it happened.'' He signaled the coachman. ''Take us to West
Smithfield.''

As the coach rumbled past St. Bartholomew's
Hospital, Annesley said, ''No one knows what would
have happened to England if Edward had lived, for
he was a true Christian. But he died when he was only
sixteen. He was then followed to the throne by his half-
sister, Mary—daughter of Catherine of Aragon.

"Mary was the worst queen England ever had. John Knox called her Bloody Queen Mary, and John Knox was right! She hated—no, she loathed Protestantism, and she vowed that she would take England back to Rome."

The coachman halted his vehicle at the side of a tiny park in West Smithfield and opened the door.

"This is the place," said Annesley. "For centuries it's been used for games and contests." He swept his arms around, indicating the large open space. "Armored knights have jousted here. But in our time it is more famous for being the place where the Bloody Queen burned Protestants.

"Poor Mary was a troubled woman. Though queen, her life was full of disappointments. Her father divorced her mother. Philip II of Spain married her, but he refused to live with her. She began a war with France and lost. She turned her wrath on Protestants. She hated the laws of her brother, which favored Protestants, and cancelled them at the first opportunity. Then she went after the Protestants. Come, let me show you where her first victim was burned."

Dr, Annesley led Susanna to a place in front of a small shop. "Tradition says that this was the spot. The date was Monday, February 4, 1555. Her victim was John Rogers, a distinguished scholar and a vicar at St. Sepulchre's." Annesley pointed to the probable path Rogers had followed.

"As the old man was led to the stake, he passed his wife and eleven children. After he had been chained to the stake, the sheriff said, 'If you will change your religion, you will save your life.' Rogers, however, had just quoted the Fifty-first Psalm and was prepared. And even though he could see his wife, with their children huddling around her, his voice was as

clear as a trumpet. 'That which I have preached, I will seal with my blood.'

"The torch was then applied to the straw and wood stacked around his feet. Mercifully, the wood was dry and he died quickly."

Susanna viewed the scene. "It's hard to believe that anyone could be so cruel!" With great effort, she asked, "How many did Queen Mary burn?"

"She executed at least three hundred. But they weren't all burned. Some were hanged; others beheaded. Mary was vicious. Among those she burned was her brother's friend, Archbishop Cranmer. The day after his death, she made Cardinal Pole the Archbishop of Canterbury. Pole was a favorite and did her bidding. She even ordered him to dig up her father's bones and burn them!"

"You mean the bones of Henry VIII?" Susanna winced.

"That's right."

"Why would she do that?"

"Because she considered him a heretic!"

On the way back to St. Giles, Susanna was quiet until the coach entered the open space around the church. Then she asked, "Why did John Rogers refuse to change his faith when he faced the fire?"

"Because Christ was extremely dear to him."

"And what was his faith?"

"Church of England."

"Then there are members of our church who really know Christ?"

"Of course! There are members of all Christian faiths and opinions who know Christ, and to whom Christianity is more than politics. But let's get back to the Bloody Queen.

"Mary died unexpectedly on November 17, 1558. And, strangely, Cardinal Pole died twelve hours later.

"Queen Elizabeth, daughter of Anne Boleyn, was a great improvement over Mary. She was a Protestant and ruled for almost half a century."

"Was she a *real* Protestant, or just a political Protestant?" asked Susanna.

"I'm afraid she was just a political Protestant. Like her half sister, she burned some who didn't agree with her."

Susanna and her father had just entered St. Giles when she began to hold her side. "I'm afraid I'm not feeling too well," she said.

"Then we'd better go home. I had hoped to tell you about my ministry here, but I can do that later."

The coachman had just lifted his whip when an old blind man and his wife shuffled up to the coach.

"Please, sir," mumbled the old man, "me and wife ain't 'ad nothin' to eat for better 'n three days." He held out a dented cup.

After frantically searching through his pockets, Annesley said, "Sorry. I'm afraid I don't even have a farthing."

"And I don't have any money either," wailed Susanna. The couple started to leave, and then Susanna's face brightened. "Robert," she said to the coachman, "could you lend me a shilling?"

"Thank you, miss," said the old lady after the coin had clinked in the cup. "That was mighty sweet."

On the return to Spital Yard, neither Susanna nor her father spoke. The only sounds that broke the silence were the noises of the high spoked wheels as they crossed the bumps, the swish of the snow, and the rhythmic clatter of the horses' hoofs. But in her head, Susanna kept hearing the tingling sound of the coin as it fell into the beggar's cup. Also, a memory of the old woman's toothless smile lingered with her.

Just as Susanna was preparing to go to her room,

she remembered her father's reference to the Declaration of Indulgence of 1672. "What was it?" she asked.

"In 1665 Parliament passed the *Five Mile Act*. This bill meant that no dissenting minister was allowed to go within five miles of any church where he had preached. Since I had been vicar at St. Giles, I was not allowed in that vicinity. The Declaration of Indulgence of 1672 cancelled that law. It was because of that cancellation that I was allowed to take you there today."

On the Rim
of the Action

While returning from the Sunday morning service
at the neighborhood Church of England, Susanna's
conscience troubled her. Just as she side-stepped a
puddle, a line from one of her father's sermons lodged
in her head. In her mind's eye she saw him in the
pulpit and heard him say: "A scruple in the mind is
as gravel in the shoe, it vexeth the conscience."

Those words now bit into her heart. It seemed she
had a pebble in each shoe. Within minutes she would
be facing him. What would she say? Keeping the *Book
of Common Prayer* out of sight under her coat, she
opened the door of their house, slipped down the hall,
and hid it under the bed. As she prepared for dinner, the tantalizing smell of roast beef filled the air.

Standing before the mirror, Susanna pushed the
comb through her hair and brushed her ankle-length,
black skirt. The Church of England service had indeed
been different! The bright vestments, the chanting,
the intermittent kneeling, the colored windows, the
candles, the high altar, and the reading of prayers

was something new. True, the vicar's sermon was not as interesting as one preached by her father. Still, she had enjoyed the service.

After a final stroke with her comb, Susanna went down to the dining room. Altogether, Dr. Annesley had had twenty-five children. Samuel, his first wife's only child, was in India. Many of the two dozen by his second wife had either died or moved away. Those who remained stood around the table and joined hands while Dr. Annesley prayed, "We thank Thee, God, for the food of which we are about to partake."

Following Puritan ideals, the Annesleys did as little work as possible on Sunday. Most of the food had been prepared the day before. Sunday was a day to worship, meditate, and rest. Family devotions were required. Each member of the family was to spend as much time reading the Bible as was spent in recreation.

The news around the crowded table that day concerned Elizabeth and John Dunton's plans to marry that summer.

But then the topic of conversation shifted. "I've heard that King Louis XIV has been tampering with the *Edict of Nantes*," announced one of the girls.

"And that's something we should pray about!" said Annesley, shaking his head.

"Why? What does that mean?" asked several.

"The Edict of Nantes is an agreement that was signed by Louis XIV's grandfather, Henry IV, with the Huguenots. They were French Christians who lived a hundred years ago. In England we call them Protestants. It allowed them freedom of worship in certain French cities. Please remember that John Calvin was French, and that there have been many Huguenots." He sighed. "I'm afraid we're facing troubled times. As you know, Louis XIV and Charles II are cousins!''

"And what does that mean?'' asked Susanna.

Annesley shrugged. "It could mean trouble. Just last week a minister friend of mine right here in London was fined 850 pounds for merely conducting a public meeting. I hope he can raise the money. If he can't, he may have to go to the Tower!''

After several minutes of conversation about how Christians had persecuted one another, Susanna noticed Elizabeth. "Why are you just picking at your food?'' she asked. "Are you ill?''

"I'm not ill,'' replied Elizabeth in a low voice. "But I thought that at least one person would be interested in my wedding! Instead, all I hear is Henry IV, Louis XIV, Charles II, and Bloody Queen Mary!''

"I'm extremely interested in your wedding,'' returned Susanna. "True, John is a bit eccentric. But I admire his religious convictions and his obsession with books and publishing. Also, I like his beard. It's most becoming. I—''

Susanna's sentence was cut short by a voice from the end of the table. "When are we going to be prosperous enough to have tea?''

"Tea costs too much!'' replied Annesley. "Fifteen shillings for a pound of tea is more than we can afford. I worked it out last week. If we were to get the tea habit, we would use about forty pounds of it a year— and that would be more than our annual rent!''

"Maybe someone could persuade our brother Sam to send us some. He's making a lot of money in India and could afford it,'' put in Elizabeth.

"Plain water is much better,'' said Annesley. "And besides, it's cheaper!''

Turning to Elizabeth, Susanna asked, "When is your wedding?''

"August 3. It will be at Allhallows the Wall. Father will preach the sermon. And do you know who else will be there?"

"Who?"

"A special friend of John Dunton," Elizabeth's voice teased.

"What's his name?"

"Oh, he's a very handsome young man."

"I'm sure of that. Dunton likes quality. But what's his name?"

"He's a most remarkable young man," Elizabeth went on. "He's brilliant, dedicated, well-educated, ambitious, strong."

"We assume all of that," said Susanna. "But, please, can't you tell me his name?"

"His name is Samuel Wesley!"

"Yes, I've met him." Susanna nodded. "He comes from a long line of Dissenters, but now he goes to the Church of England."

"And he's interested in everything that's obscure," threw in Dr. Annesley. "I once discussed with him the problems the fourth-century church had in dating Easter. To my amazement, he knew all about the Council of Nicaea. He talked about Arius, Eusebius of Caesarea, and Athanasius as if he knew them personally. I wouldn't be surprised but what he could rattle off the names of all the bishops who attended. He should write a dictionary. I think he's a genius."

"But he's stubborn!" said Elizabeth, focusing her words in the general direction of Susanna. "He and John were having coffee in Smith's Coffeehouse in George Yard when a fat colonel sitting by the fireplace began to swear. He took the Lord's name in vain again and again and soiled the air with dirty oaths.

"This was too much for Sam Wesley. After filling a large cup with water, he summoned a waiter. Then

raising his voice so that everyone in the room could
hear, he said, 'Take this water to the gentleman in
the red coat, and ask him to wash out his mouth.'

"The colonel almost exploded. He jumped to his
feet, yanked out his sword, and strode forward. If it
had not been for the soldiers who were sitting with
the colonel, there would have been a fight. John said
it was one of the funniest sights he had ever seen."

"Good for Sam!" cheered Annesley. "I admire
men of courage. But now that we've finished eating,
let us pray."

Obediently, the entire family pushed their chairs
back from the table. Each knelt by a chair; and each,
from the oldest to Susanna, prayed. Mixed in with
each prayer were words of praise, thanksgiving, and
petitions. Not one sounded formal or memorized, as
it would have if it had originated in the *Book of Common
Prayer*.

Immediately after family worship, Dr. Annesley
motioned for Susanna to follow him. In the study, he
picked up a slender volume. "Found it last week,"
he said. "It was written by your grandfather, John
White, during the Cromwell War. And since we've
been discussing recent history of the church, I thought
you'd be interested."

"Looks interesting," murmured Susanna, backing
out the door. "I'll give you a report when I'm
finished."

Reading the book was like examining a sewer. Each
of the one hundred Church of England priests seemed
more vile than the previous one. None had morals.
Many were drunkards. The majority were more interested in chasing the hounds than working in the
parish. Some collected money from several parishes
but left all of the work up to their assistants. Few

seldom, if ever, preached the gospel. A number were gamblers.

After Susanna finished the book, she went outside for fresh air. A thin layer of snow covered the ground, but the air had a tang to it. Twice as she wandered in a southerly direction she was almost drenched when pails of slop were dumped from upstairs windows.

On the banks of the Thames, she was attracted by an overpowering stench. Following the smell, she came to a large slave ship that was being repaired. From the vantage point of a stack of brick, she had an excellent view of the deck. While she observed, several dozen blacks were led from a hold by a man waving a cat-o-nine tails. Each slave was shackled to another by a chain attached to an ankle.

As Susanna's eyes widened, a youth began to beat a drum, and the man with the whip made the slaves jump up and down to the rhythm of the beat. Noticing a ship's officer with silver buckles arching his shoes, Susanna asked, "Sir, what are they doing?"

"Mornin' exercises."

"But why that dreadful whip?"

"Because some of 'em don't want to exercise."

"Why not?"

He shrugged. "They'd rather be dead than be slaves."

A fresh breeze rippled the British flag on the bow and increased the stench.

"Ugh! The smell is terrible."

The man lifted his hands in a gesture of despair. "For a girl you sure have a lot to say. The smell ain't half as bad as it was. I've smelled slavers five miles away! Reason is we don't have proper sanitary facilities. When we loaded at Benin we had six hundred slaves. There was only one bucket for every twenty. On the way about a third of 'em died and we

had to toss 'em overboard. Now there's a bucket for every fifteen or so. Things will improve by the time we get to Jamaica, for at least a third of these will die on the way over.''

Susanna shuddered. ''What you say turns my stomach. How can England call itself a Christian nation and engage in the slave trade?''

''That ain't no problem! Look at it this way, Miss. Those who get to Jamaica will become civilized. Some of 'em may even become Christians. That's why this ship's called John the Baptist. I own ten percent of her.''

Losing control, Susanna snapped, ''Are you a Christian?''

''Certainly. I was baptised when I was an infant just like everyone else in England. I've even been to church twice, and I've taken communion.''

Susanna returned home and climbed the steps to her father's study. ''Sir, were things really as bad during the civil war period as Grandfather White described them in his book?'' she asked.

Annesley smiled. ''First you must remember that your grandfather was a very outspoken man. I'll never forget how terrified I was to ask him for your mother's hand. He was a graduate of Oxford, a Puritan lawyer, a member of Parliament—and he was a dramatic man. His pen was like a sword.''

''But, sir, were the vicars he wrote about really that corrupt?''

''They were. During that period eight thousand clergymen lost their churches because of their corruption.'' He shook his head and rubbed his chin. ''I knew many of them. One was often found drunk in the vestibule of his church. Another got his appointment by bribing the king. Then he collected commissions from the preachers to whom he assigned parishes.''

Susanna bit her lip. "Does this mean that the resurrected Christ has no power?"

"Certainly not! Jesus said, 'All power is given unto me in heaven and in earth.' "

"Does that mean all—*all*—power?"

"It does."

"Then, sir, why have professed Christians done such horrible things? I've read about the Crusades, the religious wars, the persecutions, the intolerance. And I've seen with my own eyes where Bloody Queen Mary burned so many!' "

"They've done those terrible things because they have neglected the more important things: the resurrection of Jesus, His death on the cross, prayer, His Second Coming. Instead, they've concentrated on trivia. The Puritans fussed because members of the Church of England kneel when they take communion."

"And what's wrong with kneeling?"

"Because when Jesus served the first communion in the Upper Room the apostles obviously did not kneel. Instead, they sat at the table."

"Or reclined on couches like the Romans," put in Susanna.

Annesley laughed. "Next Sunday I'm going to preach on this subject. My text will be Matthew 23:23: 'Woe unto you, scribes and Pharisees, hypocrites! for ye pay tithe of mint and cummin, and have omitted the *weightier* matters of the law, judgment, mercy, and faith: these ye ought to have done, and not to leave the other undone.' "

He stood and paced the room. "What we need, Sukey, is for someone—just anyone—to light a candle in our present darkness and to lift it high enough for everyone to see the way. Such a person could change England, and changing England could change the world.'' He sighed and placed a hand on each of Susanna's shoulders. ''Lighting such a candle and holding it high will be no easy task. It would be like keeping a candle burning in the midst of a hurricane.''

''But would that be possible?'' asked Susanna.

''With people, by themselves, it would be impossible. But with God, all things are possible!''

And the Clock Ticked On

Susanna acquired the habit of going to her room each day, closing the door, reading the *Book of Common Prayer*, studying the Bible, and lingering on her knees. Her daily prayer was, "Dear God, guide me. Help me do Thy will. Make my life count."

Paul had been directed by a vision. Moses had been inspired by the burning bush. And being willing to do whatever God commanded, Susanna felt that God's directions to her would be as definite as those of an architect. But although she was always conscious of God's presence when she prayed, it seemed that the only instructions she received were: *Wait!*

Elaborate preparations had been made for Elizabeth's wedding on August 3. And among the guests was Samuel Wesley. Samuel brought an unusual gift—a poem of his own composition which he had grandly named *Epithalmium*. At the proper time, and with a magnificent flourish, he handed his gift to the bride and groom.

"So you're a poet!" exclaimed Susanna.

"I really want to be a minister," replied Samuel, obviously pleased. "But poetry is my second love. William Shakespeare is my favorite poet."

Before the day ended, Sukey and Sam had shared a long walk, had started addressing each other by first names—and had discussed their ancestors. Their forbears had tended to be nonconformists, and were deeply religious. Strangely, each of their maternal grandfathers was named John White.

"I wonder if they're related," said Samuel, a slight note of concern in his deep voice.

"If they have the same name they couldn't be related."

"You're quite right," replied Sam, his face brightening.

"What difference would it make?"

"Well, I wouldn't want to be related to you. At least not in *that* way!"

"Maybe we'd better chart our families."

Sam laughed. "I saw your chart on Henry VIII, and it was good. Yes, let's chart our relatives and compare them."

Just before they parted, Susanna learned that Samuel was studying the ins and outs of the Church of England and Nonconformity. "I haven't made up my mind which group has the most truth," he said at the door. "But I do like the Church of England!"

Three days after Elizabeth's wedding, Susanna was awakened from a nap by loud pounding on the door. Opening it, she faced a pair of officers.

"And what can I do for you?" asked Susanna, making an effort to sound calm.

"Is this the home of Dr. Annesley?" asked the one with the eyebrow moustaches.

"It is."

"Then stand aside! We have orders to seize enough

of the Doctor's belongings to pay his fine for preachin' without bein' ordained by the Church of England.''

As Susanna watched, the men ransacked the living room. They unhooked paintings, rolled up the best rugs, took her father's favorite chair, carried out both tables, and helped themselves to the best pewter.

Horrified, Susanna all but shouted, ''Isn't that enough?''

''We gotta be certain—''

''But the pewter you took was a wedding gift. Mother will be brokenhearted.''

''Don't make no difference. We've had orders from the court!'' they shouted over their shoulders.

When Annesley returned home from St. Bartholomew's Hospital where he had been visiting a sick parishoner, he viewed the wreckage in dismay.

''And what are you going to do about it?'' wailed Mrs. Annesley. ''That pewter belonged to my mother!''

''There's nothing that can be done. Charles II is our king, and he dislikes Dissenters. But don't worry. So far I haven't been sent to the Tower.''

Susanna felt a pang of guilt. Here she was living in her father's home, and was forced to watch helplessly as members from her own church took his most prized possessions and wrecked his house.

Was this a sign from the Lord? Dismayed, she fled to her room and knelt by her bed.

That evening Susanna had little appetite. Would her father scold her for attending the Church of England? Instead of scolding her, he mentioned that he had met her pastor, Dr. John Brown, at the hospital. ''He's a fine man,'' said Annesley. ''I'm sure he wouldn't agree with what happened today.''

The religious and political storms that had started long before Susanna's birth continued to darken her adolescent years. One followed the other. The hangmen at Tyburn kept busy and so did the axmen at the Tower. And now in 1685—her sixteenth year—the fury of the storms had so increased, rumors of impending war spread.

"Blood will run deep," prophesied many.

A new act in the royal drama began on Sunday, February 1, of that year. After a coach ride, dinner, and a visit with Louise, a current mistress, Charles II was escorted to his room. On the way, the candle in the attendant's hand went out. And since there was no wind, this was considered a bad omen.

The next morning His Majesty's face was pale and his speech was slightly blurred. Then, as he settled in his chair for his morning shave, he slumped on the attendant's arm. Alarmed, a court physician withdrew sixteen ounces of blood from the king's arm. In doing this, he risked being hanged, for he had not been authorized by the Council, but he thought it was the way to cure the king.

Knowing that history was trembling on the verge of a drastic turn, James, the king's brother and titled the Duke of York, scurried into the room. In his haste, he appeared with a shoe on one foot and a slipper on the other. By this time, official permission had been received for treatment and the royal bed was surrounded by twelve doctors. They shaved his head, toasted his scalp with red-hot irons, drew another six ounces of blood, forced dozens of medicines down his throat, administered enemas, burned his feet, and squirted drugs up his nose. They also covered him with blisters.

While the medical men sweated to save the king's life, British ports were sealed. In strategic places, guards were doubled.

Soon the room was crowded with those concerned

about His Majesty's soul. Among these was Anglican Bishop Thomas Ken, a former royal chaplain. He urged the king to take communion. The king refused. At this point, Queen Catherine approached James and suggested that he summon a Catholic priest. Bending low, James exchanged whispers with his brother. James then disappeared.

In the meantime, totally unaware that a Catholic priest was being sought, the Archbishop of Canterbury and the bishops of Durham, London, and Ely, joined Bishop Ken in a circle around the stricken man. Ken read the Prayer for the Sick from the *Book of Common Prayer*. By Thursday, in spite of the estimated fifty-eight medicines which had been administered, the king began to sink so rapidly it was apparent he would not recover.

Outside, church bells tolled.

Within those tense hours, Father Huddleston, disguised in a wig and cassock, waited hidden in a closet near the king's chamber. Soon, James cleared the chamber with an order: "Gentlemen, the king wishes everyone to retire."

The room having been cleared, Father Huddleston stepped out of the closet. From within his cassock, he produced the hidden crucifix. Charles II made his confession, took communion, was given Extreme Unction, and was accepted into the Roman Catholic Church.

Charles II died on Friday, February 6, 1685. It was the day of a full moon and he was in his fifty-fifth year.

Since Charles II's wife, Catherine, had no children, the closest heir was his brother James, the Duke of York. And so James, avowed Catholic though he was, became James II. At the time of his coronation on April 23, he was fifty-two.

Shortly after the coronation of James II, Samuel

Wesley visited the Annesley home. During the evening meal, he sat beside Susanna.

"Do you think England will become Catholic?" asked Dr. Annesley as he dipped into his pudding.

"I doubt it," replied Samuel.

"But during his first Sunday in power James openly attended Mass."

"True. But on the day Charles died, James assured the Privy Council that he would always defend and take care of the Church of England."

"I still have doubts," said Annesley, lifting his hands in a gesture of helplessness. "When he served as Lord High Admiral, he learned the use of deception. In my opinion, he can lie as well as Charles II lied—and Charles II was an expert."

"Be careful what you say!" warned Susanna. "I don't want you to end up in the Tower."

After a long silence, Samuel said, "His Majesty is for toleration. He said so and I believe it. Think of the thousands of Dissenters and Quakers he has just freed from prison."

"And people who follow the Pope," added Annesley, striking the table with his fist.

"Yes," agreed Samuel.

Somewhat alarmed at this conversation, Susanna nodded to the servants to start clearing the table.

That night, sitting across from one another, Susanna and Samuel visited alone by candlelight.

"Father is a little determined," apologized Susanna.

"And so am I!" replied Samuel, his deep voice resonant with confidence. "But that's as it should be. Your father, Susanna, is a brilliant man."

While they visited, Samuel produced a package. "It's for you."

Eyes sparkling, Susanna opened it with care. Then

she held up a new book. It was titled: *Maggots; or Poems on several Subjects never before handled by a Scholar.*

"I wrote it," he said, "and it's for you." He eagerly studied her face as she viewed his portrait in the front. The woodcut showed him crowned with laurel and with a maggot perched on his forehead.

"But why did you call it *Maggots*?"

"Read the poem beneath the picture and you'll see."

Slowly and carefully Susanna read:

> In our own defence the author writes,
> Because when this foul maggot bites,
>   He ne'er can resist in quiet:
> Which makes him so sad a face,
> He'd beg your worship, or your grace,
>   Insight, unseen, to buy it.

"Here, let me autograph it for you," he said. With a proud swing, he wrote, "For Susanna Wesley, Princess of the Rectory." He added, "With love," and signed his name.

Susanna held the book next to her heart. "I'll treasure it the rest of my life," she said. "I'll read every word."

A note in the book indicated that it had been printed for John Dunton "at the sign of the Black Raven, near the Royal Exchange." It was dated 1685. At the time, Samuel Wesley was nineteen.

"What about that chart tracing your genealogy?" asked Susanna.

"I was too excited about *Maggots* to get it done. But I'll prepare one. Then we can compare it with yours so that we can make certain that we're not related." He laughed.

"And why shouldn't we be related?" Susanna touched her hair.

"Well, mmmm. Well, that might cause complica-
tions. Your're such a nice girl I'd hate to think I was
related to you!"

He glanced at the clock.

"But you haven't told me what you're doing, and
how you, a Dissenter, can be attending Oxford," said
Susanna.

"That's an interesting story. But it's a long one.
I'll tell you all about it the next time I come."

As they shook hands at the door, Samuel held her
hand tighter than usual. While they lingered with their
hands clasped, the barking of a dog, followed by the
shrill growls of a pair of tomcats filled the air. Finally
Samuel withdrew his hand and broke the awkward
moment by saying, "Pray for me."

Susanna watched as he turned the corner in the
bright moonlight. Then she picked up the book,
selected five or six long candles, and went to her room.
Maggots contained 172 pages, and she was determined
to read each page at least once.

The poetry was not really great. Still, Samuel was
just beginning to write. If he could continue to write,
maybe in a few years—But would the world hold
together for the next few years? While thoughts of
approaching trouble clouded her mind, she knelt for
prayer, and then pinched out the candle.

In September, Samuel visited again at the Annesley
home. "You keep asking why I'm going to Oxford,"
he said as he sat next to Susanna on a bench in the
park. "As you know, my blood flows with dissent.
For generations my ancestors were Dissenters. Also,
I attended two of their schools before I started at
Oxford."

"How can you go to Oxford and be a Dissenter?"
asked Susanna.

"You can't. All universities are closed to anyone

who isn't a member of the Church of England. King James, of course, will change that so Catholics can be admitted.''

"And so you've become an Anglican?''

"Yes, I guess we're both Anglicans! But, Susanna, neither of us should forget our rich heritage. The Church of England needs to learn many things from the Dissenters. The Dissenters have truths the world needs to hear!''

"And what do you think of the dreadful things King James has been doing?''

Samuel shuddered. "I don't know. I don't approve of bloodshed. Still, he is our king; and Paul told us to be subject unto the higher powers.''

"Even though the man is a tyrant?''

"Yes, even though he is a tyrant.''

As Susanna and Samuel walked home hand in hand, Susanna had a question. "Don't you have doubts about the rightness of leaving the Dissenters and attending Oxford?''

"Absolutely not. I prayed about it for days before making the break, for I want to do exactly what God wants me to do. Before I went to Oxford I lived with my mother and an old aunt. Both were penniless. And both were as filled with dissent as John Bunyan! But I refused to let their views hinder me. At that time, all I had was forty-five shillings. And since this wasn't enough to pay my way to Oxford by stage, I walked. At Oxford I registered at Exetor College as a servitor.''

Susanna frowned. "What's that?''

"A servitor is a student who waits on another: shines his shoes, mails his letters, carries his books, makes his bed. When I entered, I listed myself as a *pauper scholaris*. I've made my own way. The Lord has opened doors. Now I have more money than when

I started! I earned it writing articles—and tutoring."

"When will you finish?"

"I'll have my B.A. degree in June, 1688."

"Then what?"

"I'll apply for ordination."

Susanna bit her lip, and cocked her head to one side. "Do you think the world will last that long?"

"It had better!" exclaimed Sam.

The Storm Darkens

At the Annesley table one day, about the time the soup was served, the conversation turned to the subject of John Dunton.

"If he doesn't pay his debts soon he'll end up in debtor's prison," said one at the table. "Elizabeth is so worried she can't sleep."

"I was afraid John was expanding too fast," commented Annesley, as he buttered a slice of bread. Then with a mischievous look at Susanna, he added, "Maybe he invested too much in *Maggots*."

"No. That's not the problem," said Susanna. "That book is doing well. Orders are coming in. There may be a second printing! Other books have slowed."

Susanna went on. "I have something else to say. It's important and I want to make sure there are no spies around."

"Speak, the servants can be trusted," said Dr. Annesley.

Dropping her voice to a hoarse whisper, Susanna

said, "Sam has been very much attached to James
II. King James *is* a brave man. He risked his life blowing up houses to help stop the progress of the Great
Fire. He was a distinguished admiral. New York City
was named in his honor when he was the Duke of
York. And he's a Stuart and is thus entitled to the
throne regardless of his religion. But something is
going on at Oxford that is changing Sam's opinion.

"Right after the coronation, King James appointed
a Catholic, dean of Oxford's Christ Church. He also
licensed Obadiah Walker to publish Papist books.
Some fear James II wants to turn Oxford into a Papist
university!"

As she spoke, her father thoughtfully rubbed his
chin. Then he said, "Up 'till now, James has done
a lot of good. He's freed thousands of Quakers and
Dissenters from prison; and rumor is that he has
donated 500 pounds to help the Huguenots who
escaped. Also I know, for I saw a copy, that he issued
a bulletin which he ordered read in all churches. That
paper requested aid for the Huguenots. As for me,
I'm going to believe in him, even though he is a
Papist. His Majesty James II is our king!"

Three and a half weeks later Dunton sailed for
America. "Hate to leave Liz," he confided to
Susanna. "But if I don't pay my debts—" He stroked
his beard. "If I don't pay my debts I'll be locked up."

Susanna and Sam began taking long walks. They
visited parks; watched men working on the reconstruc-
tion of St. Paul's; and visited Pudding Lane where
the Great London Fire started. They also visited Pie
Corner where the conflagration reached its zenith.
While sitting within the shadows of London Bridge,
the conversation turned to politics.

"As it is now," said Sam, placing a finger
lengthwise on his palm, "James II will be followed

by his oldest daughter Mary. She will become Mary
II. But if Mary should pass away before her father,
the throne will go to Anne.''

"That means the new queen will be Roman
Catholic.''

"Wrong.''

"Oh, but I'm not wrong!'' replied Susanna flatly.
"Either daughter will be Catholic because James II
is Catholic; and his first wife, Anne Hyde, mother
of both Mary and Anne, was Catholic.''

"Your logic is correct,'' admitted Sam, tapping his
palm with his finger. "But you're forgetting one thing.
Providence! God is running this world whether we
believe it or not. In the end He will have His way.''
He laid two fingers in his palm. "True, Mary and
Anne's roots are Catholic. Nonetheless, Charles II,
Catholic though he is, forced his brother James to raise
them as Protestants. James was angry about that, but
since Charles II outranked him, he had no choice.''

Susanna shook her head. "That's amazing. But are
Mary and Anne *really* and *truly* Protestant?''

"Yes, they are *really* and *truly* Protestant. My friend,
Dr. Henry Compton, Bishop of London, tutored
them. He's an excellent teacher.''

"Then our next ruler could be Protestant?''

"That's the way it looks now. Mary is queen-
apparent. But there are problems. First of all, Mary
is married to her cousin, William of Orange, and if
Mary became queen, William might insist on being
crowned king. That could happen even though he is
a Holland-Dutchman, for William *is* Protestant!'' He
stood and pulled Susanna to her feet. "Let's look at
the bridge. Then on our way to Spital Square we can
get something to eat. I have something important I
want to discuss with you.''

"You said that there are two problems with the succession; but you only mentioned one."

"The other problem is very simple," he said, taking her by the hand. "And that problem is that Mary of Modena, our present queen, may have a son. If she does, he will be the heir."

"But all of Mary's children have died."

"True. Still, a new one might live."

The narrow stone bridge crossing the Thames was supported by a series of stone arches, making the full length of the bridge nine hundred and ten feet. "It was built in the late twelfth century," explained Samuel, speaking like a guide. "It was built by a preacher. His name was Peter. He was chaplain of St. Mary Colechurch in the City."

As they crossed the bridge, they came to a tunnel-like enclosure. This was created by a long series of three-story and four-story buildings on each side of the bridge. These buildings were only twelve feet wide. A mere four feet of each rested on the bridge; the other eight feet projected above the river. Thus, the passageway itself was a scant twelve feet wide.

Across the centuries, numerous buildings had slipped into the river. But since the buildings on one side were attached to those on the other side, slippage was uncommon. In 1358 there were one hundred and thirty-eight houses or shops on the bridge; and, according to legend, King John (1167-1216) decreed that the taxes from this property should pay for the upkeep of the bridge.

Toward the southward bank, they came to the drawbridge. "It used to resemble the tower of an ancient castle," explained Sam. He pointed to a Dutch tower made of wood and decorated with gilded weathervanes. As Susanna followed his finger, she

suddenly shuddered. "Look, Sam. Look! That bearded skull is staring at us! Ugh!"

"Yes, that's Jenkins. Robbed an old woman. He was executed last week. The skulls are mounted as a warning. Centuries ago, the old stone tower was topped with them. From a distance they looked like Catholic prayer beads. One was that of Sir Thomas More, author of *Utopia*. He was Catholic and because he disagreed with Henry VIII for divorcing Catherine, Henry had his head chopped off. Sir Thomas was a great man."

As the sky darkened, a brilliant streak of forked lightning cut through the air; and a moment later a sharp clap of thunder shook the bridge. Pulling her coat a little tighter, Susanna studied a trio of barges pushing up the Thames.

"Did a cat get your tongue?" asked Samuel.

"It's going to rain," she replied. "And I was

wondering about the bridge. It's the only bridge in London that crosses the Thames. If it should be destroyed, the only way to cross the river would be by boat or ferry; and then London would again be divided.'' She was silent for a dozen steps or so, and then she said rather fiercely, "Why do men have to load the bridge with all those horrible buildings and keep on decorating it with human skulls? We are in the seventeenth century! This is the age of enlightenment! Newton has discovered the laws of gravity. Harvey has proved that blood circulates. Galileo has discovered the moons of Jupiter. Can we, with such knowledge, put up with such dreadful sights?''

"But it takes time to learn. Remember the story of the compass?''

"I remember. But those dreadful sights on London Bridge are not the only things that horrify me. Doesn't the Bible say that Christ is the only way to salvation?''

"It does. Acts 4:12 is quite clear; 'Neither is there salvation in any other: for there is no other name under heaven among men, whereby we must be saved.' ''

"In other words, just as London Bridge is the only way across the Thames, Christ's way is the only way to heaven. Is that right?''

"That's correct, as your father would say.''

"Then why do we make Christianity so difficult? We have disputes over things that are not even mentioned in the New Testament! Catholics, Dissenters, Anglicans all believe that Christ is the only way. Then why do Catholics burn Protestants, and Protestants burn Catholics, and Dissenters tear up the *Book of Common Prayer*, and wreck cathedrals that have taken centuries to build?''

"Sukey!'' said Samuel. "You're not only Dr.

Annesley's twenty-fifth child, you are also a barrel
of gunpowder! As you were talking , I was wondering what would happen if we got married. People say
that I'm as stubborn as King John.''

"And they're right! You *are* as stubborn as King
John.'' She shook her head and buttoned up her coat.
"But as stubborn as King John was, he signed Magna
Carta!''*

"True. But he was forced to sign it.''

"And who forced him to sign it?''

"The nobles.''

"And who was the spiritual power behind the
nobles?''

"Stephen Langton, Archbishop of Canterbury.''

"And what was Langton's denomination?''

"Well, that was before the Reformation, and so he
was Catholic.''

"And who inspired Langton?'' Susanna's voice had
an edge to it.

"The Holy Spirit.''

"And that,'' said Susanna with conviction, "proves
to us that God is still running this world! He influences
Protestants, Catholics, and every type of Dissenter.''

"You're right, Sukey. But remember, Langton was
a *man*.''

"True. Langton was a man. But please remember
he was brought into this world by a woman, and that
Jesus Christ was brought into this world by a woman,
and that Moses was brought into this world by a
woman. Also, remember Langton was the one who
divided the Bible into chapters.''

---

* Signed at Runnymede on June 15, 1215, the *Magna Cartar*
or *Great Charter* is a foundation of democracy. One of its sixty-
three provisions reads: "No free man shall be arrested, imprisoned, outlawed, or deprived of property except by judgment of his
equals or the law of the land.''

They both laughed. A hundred or so steps later, Susanna said, "If we don't hurry we'll be soaked. It's going to pour." As they half-ran, she added, "I'm afraid that you've been reading John Knox!"

Comfortable in a candle-lit corner of a tiny restaurant on the north side of the river, Samuel ordered dinner. As they waited for the soup, he said, "I've been longing to tell you something important." He shifted a pair of tall candles closer to Susanna. "There, now I can see that determined face of yours more clearly. And I do like to look at you even though you don't approve of John Knox!" Then, pointing at the window, he remarked, "Look at that rain, and feel the wind. We made it just in time."

"Maybe the storm will blow old Jenkins' head into the river," suggested Susanna. Instead of answering, Samuel began to eat his soup. Susanna watched him spoon the soup to his mouth until the bowl was half empty. "I thought you were going to tell me something important," she said.

"Oh, excuse me." He licked his lips. "This soup is good. We don't fare this well at Oxford! The important news is that I'll be getting my degree on the nineteenth of June. Then I'll be qualified for deacon's orders." He rubbed his hands. "I've dreamed that Bishop Compton would officiate at my ordination. That would be a real reward for all my work. He is to me what Paul was to Timothy.

"But, Sukey, I'm worried." He paused to swallow several spoons of soup. "The reason I'm worried is that Compton hates Popery so much he doesn't get along with the king. Indeed, Compton may be sent to the Tower!

"Last summer His Majesty came to Oxford. I got to hear him speak. He was angry because the authorities at the university wouldn't accept all of his appointments. I can still see him. Facing his audience, his eyes seemed to burn. 'You have not dealt with me like gentlemen,' he said. 'You have been unmannerly as well as undutiful. Is this your Church of England loyalty? I could not have believed that so many clergymen of the Church of England would have been concerned with such business. Go home! Get you gone! I am king. I will be obeyed! Go to the chapel this instant, and admit the Bishop of Oxford. Let those who refuse look to it; they shall feel the weight of my hand; they shall know what it is to incur the displeasure of their sovereign!' "

As Sam quoted the king, his voice kept rising until Susanna feared that he would be overheard. "You'd better lower your voice or *you'll* end up in the Tower," she whispered, her eyes on a pair of red-coated officers sitting nearby.

Samuel's anger remained even after the lobsters were served. "You know, Sukey," he said, striking his palm with his index finger, "Truth is truth; and I'm going to stand for the whole truth, and nothing but the truth. I'm going to do that even if my head ends up on London Bridge!" He emphasized his declaration by cracking a huge lobster claw.

"You may be right, Mr. Wesley," replied Susanna. "But our good friend, William Shakespeare, said that discretion is the best part of valor."

"That's a misquote, Sukey. Shakespeare said, 'The better part of valor is discretion.' And sometimes it is. But not always—"

"I know I misquoted Shakespeare, Mr. Wesley." Susanna's fingers had almost doubled into fists. "But I think you get the point! The quote is from Henry IV, Part 1. And if you'd like to borrow the play, father has it in his study."

Samuel scowled. After dipping a large chunk of lobster into the melted butter, he said, "Sukey, you and I are as opposite as the north and south poles. Ah, but maybe that's the way Providence wants it to be! Iron sharpeneth iron." He paused, looked her full in the face, and smiled. "I, too, believe in discretion. But what would have happened if John the Baptist had always been discreet? True, he might have saved his head, but would the Kingdom of God have been advanced? My main interest in life, Sukey, is to be utterly obedient to God even if I'm sent to the Tower and beheaded!"

By the time they had finished dinner, the rain had stopped. They headed for Spital Square. After a few blocks, their hands came together, and each felt a responsive squeeze from the other.

The grandfather clock was booming nine when Susanna stepped through the front door of her father's house. "This has been a most exciting day," said Dr. Annesley after Susanna had removed her coat. "King James has issued a new proclamation of indulgence that is worrying a lot of people. The vicar of your church was over this afternoon. He's very concerned."

"What's the problem?"

"This new declaration is almost a duplicate of the one he issued in Scotland last year, and that one really stirred up a lot of trouble. Here, let me read it to you. It starts out, '*We, by our sovereign authority, prerogatives royal, and absolute power —* ' " He shook his head. "That, Sukey, assumes a lot of power. And please notice, he never mentioned Parliament. Not once!"

"And why not?"

"Because King James never consulted Parliament. But let me read the rest of the proclamation. 'We allow and tolerate moderate Presbyterians to meet in their

private houses, and to hear such ministers as have
been, or are willing to accept our indulgence, but they
are *not* to build meetinghouses, but to exercise in
houses. We tolerate Quakers to meet in their form
in any place, or places, appointed for their worship;
and we by our *sovereign authority*, suspend, stop, and
disable, all laws or Acts of Parliament made or executed against any of our Roman Catholic subjects,
so that they may be free to exercise their religion.' "

Dr. Annesley took a deep breath, then continued.
"Protestants are saying that this indulgence is illegal
because it was not passed by Parliament, and that its
main purpose is to remove the restrictions against
Catholics."

"And allow Catholics to attend the universities and
have rank in the army?" asked Susanna.

"Correct! The king has asked all Protestant
clergymen to read their copy of the indulgence to their
congregations next Sunday."

"Are you going to read it?"

"No."

"Then you may be arrested?"

"Perhaps. We may even have another civil war."
Then Annesley added, "But whatever happens, may
God have His way!"

Lightning

As Monday's breakfast neared its end, Dr. Annesley turned to Susanna. "Did Dr. Brown read the king's proclamation?"

"Never mentioned it." said Susanna. "But he did pray for the king."

Annesley shrugged. "I've checked around London and it seems no one read it. Robert Bench was an exception. He read it. But he didn't read it until the congregation was gone and the doors were locked! I'm afraid, Sukey, that England's headed for trouble. The torch is sputtering near the fuse. I wouldn't be surprised but what some of the brethren will go into hiding. May God help us!"

The next day, while riding with her father to St. Bartholomew's, Susanna had a question. "Sir, what do you think of John Knox?"

"Great man. Revolutionized Scotland. Turned it Presbyterian."

"But do you agree with his writings?"

Annesley laughed. "Your voice is as serious as that

of a defense lawyer at Old Bailey." He frowned. "Could it be that you've just read *First Blast of the Trumpet Against the Monstrous Regiment of Women*?"

"Yes, and it's horrible!" She unfolded a sheet of paper. "I copied some of his statements so that I could ask you about them. Here's one: 'To promote a woman to bear rule, superiority, dominion of empire above any realm, nation, or city, is repugnant to nature, contumely'—I looked that up and it means insulting—'to God, a thing most contrarious to his revealed will and approved ordinance.' " She shuddered. "And here's another quote. 'Women are weak, frail, impatient, feeble, foolish, inconstant'—that means fickle—'cruel and lacking in the spirit of counsel and judgment.' "

Susanna folded the paper. "Sir, if women are that dreadful, how can I accomplish anything? I want to fulfill God's will for my life. I want my life to count!"

Annesley smiled. While bracing himself as the coach crossed a series of bumps and a pothole, he said, "Let's not be too hard on Brother Knox. He was a most remarkable man—even though he breathed fire and brimstone. You must remember we're all victims of our age, and Knox lived in the mid-1500's. That was a dark age! The Catholic-Protestant conflict almost scorched Scotland. Not only that, but Knox was captured by the French and made into a galley slave. He was chained to a seat in a ship and a man stood above him with a whip. Sometimes he was beaten until his back was raw. And often he was forced to keep rowing until he was utterly exhausted. But in spite of this earthly hell, he kept the faith.

"After two years in the galleys, John was released. He then moved to England and continued to preach. In those days he was terribly disturbed by what was happening to European Protestants. The ruling

women of his day tried to wipe them out. Among these
was Catherine de Medici of France. She was the wife
of Henry II and the mother of three French kings.
She's the one who instigated the St. Bartholomew
Massacre. Then there was Mary Queen of Scots, and
our own Bloody Queen Mary." He shook his head.

"John Knox called all these women Jezebels. And
he was right!" Annesley laughed and rubbed his
hands. "When he published his book, he didn't even
use his name. That would have been too dangerous!
He would have been sentenced to the stake."

"What do you believe about the book?" Susanna
studied his face.

"Knox was a little severe. Anyway, he didn't really
hate women. Most of his remaining letters were written to women. But tell me, why are you so interested
in this subject?"

"It's because I want to make my life count."

"Don't be discouraged. Although it is true that
Jesus didn't have women apostles, and there were no
women at the Last Supper, He was financially supported by women, women comforted Him at the
Cross, women wanted to prepare His body, and after
His resurrection, His first appearance was to a
woman."

"Then do you think that God could have a special
task for me?"

"Of course!"

"And when will He tell me what it is?"

"That I don't know. But He will lead you. He will
lead you by opening and closing doors. By the Word.
By the Holy Spirit. By what happens in your life. And
through prayer."

After visiting in the hospital, Dr. Annesley returned
to the carriage. His face was ashen and his lips seemed
frozen in a straight line. He jerked the door open and

signaled to the driver to take them home. "And
hurry," he said.

"What's the problem?" asked Susanna.

"I met five or six clergymen from the Church of
England, and they all told me that they have refused
to read the king's Indulgence Proclamation. One of
them told me that seven bishops are also refusing to
let their vicars read the Proclamation—"

"What does all this mean?"

"I don't know. It may mean—But I really don't
know. The one thing you and I must do is to pray."

As the carriage crunched up to the driveway in
Spital Square, Elizabeth came rushing out to meet
them. "I have wonderful news," she exclaimed.

"What is it?"

"You'll know when you go through the door!"

When Susanna stepped into the house, John
Dunton gave her a big hug. "Well, I'm home; and
I'm glad you did a good job taking care of Liz. Has
she behaved herself?"

"Of course. But what happened to your beard?"

"Shh! I still owe a lot of money and could be sent
to debtor's prison. I don't want to be recognized, and
so don't tell anyone that I'm home."

During the rest of the week, Susanna learned that
her brother-in-law had not done well in America.
Indeed, he was now worse off financially than he had
been before he left.

"And what are you going to do?" asked Dr.
Annesley.

"I really don't know. But I think that Samuel
Wesley and I will publish a magazine. He's a good
writer, and I'm a good printer. *Maggots* is still selling."

Susanna glanced at her father. But neither said a
word.

On the following Sunday, John Dunton appeared

at the door dressed as a woman. At first Susanna didn't recognize him. When she did, she said, "Why are you dressed like that?"

"I'm hungry to hear Dr. Annesley preach. Haven't heard a good sermon for so long I'm famished. Elizabeth isn't well. She couldn't come."

"But what if you're recognized?"

He shrugged. "Then I'll be sent to prison. But I won't be recognized. And if I am, I know what to do."

Upon entering the church, John took a seat in an obscure corner dark with shadows. He knew that several had recognized him; but he was confident that they would keep his secret. But on his way back to Spital Square as he was walking down Bishopsgate Street, he passed a dark-haired hoodlum of about twenty with a livid scar across his check and a green patch over his left eye.

As Dunton brushed the man, he got a whiff of gin

and noticed a flick of interest in his good eye. Forcing himself not to increase his pace, he walked on. But he had only advanced a dozen steps when the hoodlum began to take longer and then longer steps toward him.

Self-control gone, and with Scarface gaining, John began to run. Scarface did likewise, and he also began to shout, "Catch him! Catch him! That's a man in women's clothes!" Soon he was joined by others.

Heart pounding, Dunton dodged into an alley, fled between two houses, emerged in another alley, and then continued on in a long neglected street piled high with debris from the Great Fire. With expert knowledge of that section of London, he finally approached Spital Square.

Susanna was just returning from church when she saw him jerk open the door of their house and almost leap inside. But upon entering she could not find him. "John! John! Where are you?" she called. Not finding him in any of the rooms, she searched under the beds.

Half an hour later, he emerged from the kitchen closet. "They almost got me," he said.

"Who almost got you?"

John related the story and then added, "Debtor's prison is nothing to laugh about. I visited a friend in one. It was filthy, crammed with rats, spiders, cockroaches—and even human filth. The prisoners were hungry and the place stunk. It was like Dante's hell!"

"But what are you going to do now? You can't run all the time."

"I'll stay hidden until I can pay my most threatening debts. After that, I'll be safe."

As summer descended on London, the parks filled with the songs of birds, lovers walked hand-in-hand beneath the trees, hawkers sold their wares, and little knots of people whispered behind their hands. The concern was, What foolish thing will King James do next? Will there be war?

Shaken by the Proclamation of Indulgence, seven bishops met at the Archbishop's palace to discuss the issue. Their conclusion was that as members of the House of Lords, they would approach His Majesty and ask him to withdraw the proclamation.

Honoring the king as the Defender of the Faith, the fully-robed bishops faced him on their knees. The king's reaction was that of anger. While staring at Bishop Trelawny whom he dubbed "the sauciest of them all," he half shouted, "I did not expect this from your church!"

The Seven Bishops had intended their meeting with the king to be secret, but someone relayed the story to the press. This made the event a national issue. It was soon being debated throughout the United Kingdom. Eventually King James decided the Seven Bishops should be arrested, imprisoned in the Tower, and eventually tried for seditious libel—a crime that could cost them their heads.

On June 8, 1688, the Seven Bishops were placed on a barge, transported down the Thames, and locked in the Tower. Again the story of what was happening got out, and so as the barge made its way downstream, the banks were lined with masses of well-wishers who had come to cheer. As the prelates were led into the Tower, hundreds more crowded around them. Many sought their blessings or stretched out their arms, hoping to touch them.

Two days later, on Trinity Sunday, June 10, 1688, the drama of the imprisoned bishops was eclipsed by an even more startling drama. The Queen, Mary of Modena, allegedly gave birth to a son in St. James Palace.

Such a son was, of course, the new Prince of Wales,

and legal heir to the throne—surpassing both Mary and Anne. But was he genuine?

Normally, when a royal child is born, the Archbishop of Canterbury was expected to witness the birth and to sign documents indicating the birth to be genuine. But on this Sunday the Archbishop was in prison, and the responsible Protestants were in church!

Immediately doubts about the genuiness of the new "heir" began to spread. Many said that the baby was brought into the room in a brass warming-pan—that Mary wasn't even pregnant. And to prove this, maps were drawn to show how the warming-pan might have been smuggled into the room.

While the masses argued about whether the new Prince of Wales was real, lawyers prepared for the trial of the Seven Bishops which was scheduled for June 15, and Samuel Wesley prepared for his graduation four days later.

During this hectic week, Susanna spent many hours in prayer and in searching the Bible. She had a deep inward conviction that her hour of decision was at hand. Each of her prayers included the words, "Lord, help me to do Thy will." Also, she was concerned about the welfare of her father. Fearing he might be arrested, she was startled by every knock at the door.

The trial, which was conducted at Westminister Hall, lasted all day. But at 9 A.M. the next day, the jury was ready with their verdict. "Not guilty!" said the foreman. This acquittal was greeted with shouts of joy, and flowers were spread in the paths of the released men. That night, London blazed with bonfires, church bells rang, and parades, lighted by torches, thumped through the city.

The new baby was christened James Francis Edward Stuart, with complete Roman Catholic rites.

The highest Roman Catholic official in London represented the Pope as the baby's godfather. This ceremony radiated chills among the Protestants. To them, James Francis Edward was *The Pretender*—the product of a warming pan.

James Francis Edward seemed well at the time of his birth; but within six weeks his glow of health was gone. The doctors believed milk was not good for him. And so it was ordered that he should subsist on sugar, wine, water-gruel, currents, barley, and oatmeal. He had an open sore on his arm that did not heal, so special drops were prepared. These drops horrified the attendants, for when some were accidentally dropped on the tablecloth, they ate holes through it.

In all, thirty bottles lined the nursery table. The concoctions were regularly forced down the little prince's throat. But instead of responding, he worsened. In desperation, the queen ignored the doctors and summoned a woman nurse who could give milk to the baby by nursing him. This nurse, plus several more, saved his life.

The baby's health was a main topic of conversation throughout the United Kingdom. Between puffs on her pipe, a toothless old women assured her household, "All he needs is some Lady Pakenham's Tonic. It saved Isaac Newton and he weren't no bigger than a shoe. A bottle or two would make him as healthy as a cat." Another shook her head. "He ain't a-gonna live. He's Catholic and England don't need no more Catholics on the throne."

As King James' popularity sank, more and more rumors spread that Parliament would turn the throne over to his son-in-law, the Prince of Orange. At the same time, intelligence reports insisted that the Prince was assembling an invasion fleet in Holland.

Knowing that a correct wind was necessary for

William to reach England, James kept glancing out his windows at the weathercock on the Banqueting House at Whitehall.

The Prince of Orange sailed for England on October 20, 1688. His fleet consisted of two hundred transports and fifty warships. Alas, a sudden storm drove him back to Holland the next day and one of his ships sank. He was now forced to wait for a favorable wind.

The "Protestant" wind began to blow on November 1.

With banners bearing the slogan, *For Religion and Liberty*, William, the Prince of Orange, edged into the North Sea. His plans were to land in Northern England where the masses had been reported ready to unite with him. But again his fleet was dominated by winds. This time they drove him through the Strait of Dover and down the English Channel. As the winds filled his sails, William feared he might be driven into Portsmouth. Portsmouth was known to have a heavy Catholic garrison!

On November 4, however, the wind shifted to the west and blew him along the southern coast of England. While this was going on, the English fleet, stationed on the Essex coast, was trying to make it to the north, where its commanders felt William would be landing. On November 5, William of Orange stepped ashore at Brixham, on the southwest coast of England. From there, he marched in easy, unopposed stages to London. His 14,000-man army was not as large as that of his father-in-law. But it had higher morale.

William and Mary were proclaimed king and queen of the United Kingdom on February 13, 1689. And with the now-restored Dr. Robert Compton officiating, they were crowned in Westminister Abbey on April 11. Part of the agreement with Parliament was that Mary's children, if any, were next in line for the throne; and that following them, Anne, daughter of the former James II, was the heir-apparent. It was also agreed that no Catholic, or wife or husband of a Catholic, could ever occupy the throne as either king or queen.

The "Glorious Revolution" had been accomplished without the firing of a single shot. This pleased William, for he had hoped to avoid violence.

After several attempts to follow his wife and son who had escaped to France, James II tried again on December 12. Disguised in an old coat, a black wig, and a patch on the left side of his mouth, he gingerly stepped into a boat.

Louis XIV accepted James with enthusiasm, provided him with an income and a small army. Encouraged, James tried to regain his throne by invading Ireland. But he was thoroughly defeated.

Following his defeat, James returned to France where he spent the rest of his life in retirement. It was the end of the bitter conflict between Catholics and Protestants for the throne. However, it was not the end of controversy. Many felt William had no right to be king. The matter would continue to haunt the nation and the Wesley family.

As Susanna watched these lightning flashes with deep concern, her main interest remained with Samuel Wesley. Since James II had suspended Compton, Samuel was disappointed that Compton could not ordain him as a deacon. But now that William and Mary were on the throne, Compton had been returned to power. While sitting with Susanna in the living room at Spital Square, Samuel said, "Tomorrow, February 24, I'm going to be ordained a priest. And who do you think will officiate?"

"I have no idea."

"Dr. Henry Compton, the one who tutored Mary and Anne and who just crowned William and Mary."

"Oh, Sam, I'm so proud!" Susanna patted his hand. "And what are you going to do now?"

"I've been offered the chaplaincy on a man-of-war. It'll be a good place to gain experience."

"I'll miss you!" said Susanna sadly.

Later, withdrawing her hand from his, Susanna said, "I don't agree that William of Orange should be the king. According to law, the throne still belongs to James II—Catholic though he is."

Wesley stared at her. "You'd better not say that to anyone else. I'd hate to know that you had been sentenced to have that pretty little head of yours chopped off."

Susanna laughed. "Maybe you can convince me. Draw a chart that will prove that William of Orange is really a Stuart. And while you're doing that, I'll get a plate of tarts."

Using a ruler, and making quick slashes, Samuel produced a chart in minutes.

"There," he said, pointing to the drawing, "you can see that the Prince of Orange—William III—is the son of Mary, the daughter of Charles I. You can also see that King William III and his wife, Mary, the daughter of James II, are first cousins. That means that both the king and queen are Stuarts!"

"Perhaps," conceded Susanna reluctantly. "But William is half Dutch, and Protestant though he may be, he's not an Anglican!" She adjusted the knot of hair at the back of her head. "And besides, his Stuart blood comes only from the *female* side."

Samuel shook his head. "Sukey, you're even more stubborn than I am!" He wolfed a tart, then added,

"But that's all right. A magnet has to have both a
north and a south pole!"

"And which pole am I?"

"I don't know. All I know is that we don't agree
on anything, except that we both love the Lord."

"And isn't that the most important thing?"

"It is," he said, kissing her lightly on the cheek.
"I've made a chart of both our family trees. But I
forgot to bring it with me. Each of our families bris-
tle with poker-spined Dissenters. That's interesting.
But the most interesting thing is that we're not related.
You're not even a third cousin. That's wonderful."

GENEALOGY OF WILLIAM AND MARY

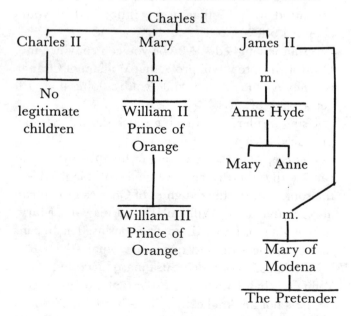

m. = married
William III married Mary, daughter of
James II. They became King William
and Queen Mary.

"Why is that wonderful?"

"Because I want to have a lot of children. Children are healthier if their parents are not related."

"Mmmm. And what does that mean?"

He held her hand in both of his, while he said, "Susanna Annesley, will you marry me?"

"Will I marry you?" Susanna repeated the words slowly and looked away. "I—I really don't know. I might, and I might not—"

The grandfather clock boomed ten, and while it was booming, Susanna lit three fresh candles. "I don't think we should be sitting in the dark, especially at this late hour," she explained.

"If you can't answer me right now, will you pray about it?" asked Samuel.

"Yes, I will pray about it," she replied, speaking slowly. "But I have a question."

"Ask it. I'm listening."

"What do you think of *First Blast of the Trumpet Against The Monstrous Regiment of Women* by John Knox?"

Samuel shrugged. "It's a rather long book."

"True. But what do you think about it?"

"It's full of strong meat—"

"But what do you think about it?"

"I'll have to re-read it. I've been too busy with Greek and Hebrew."

"But do you agree with its theme?"

Suddenly Sam's face and neck turned crimson. "I-I-I-uh really don't know."

As he said that, Dr. Annesley entered the room.

Don't Deflect Your Compass

As broad-winged gulls swerved and turned in the currents just above the ship's masts, and the tang of the sea filled his lungs, Samuel Wesley climbed onto the man-of-war to which he had been assigned.

While hurrying across the blood-red deck, he tingled with inspiration. It was great to be alive! On a moonlit night, Susanna had agreed to marry him. And she had said yes in spite of his approval of John Knox. Better yet, he was confident the poem he was planning would stand shoulder to shoulder with the best!

But there were many things he would have to learn before he could extend his wings. And now that he was chaplain of the ship, he'd have to learn them or face ridicule. Everything he saw was different.

"Why, sir, is the deck red?" he inquired of a sailor who was mending some canvas.

"It was painted red, sir, so that when we get into a fight with another ship the blood won't be so conspicuous. Before it was painted that color, the sight

of the blood encouraged the enemy and lowered our morale. Blood-red decks, sir, are an advantage.''

"Thank you, sir!" replied Wesley, forcing himself to salute for the first time in his life.

"Aye, aye, sir!" responded the man, touching his forelock.

It was then that Wesley noticed that the man's arms and chest were covered with blue tattoo marks. The design that crossed his chest was that of a huge anchor.

"And your name, sir?"

"Jim. Just call me Jim. I'm from Birmingham."

Within a week Chaplain Wesley had acquired the beginnings of a new vocabulary. He had learned that *leeward* meant the direction the wind was blowing; *forward* is toward the bow; *aft* is toward the stern. The right side of a ship is *starboard*; and the left is *port*. He also learned the names of the sails and that to *reef* one meant to reduce its size by rolling it up.

During the first week, he often found himself rushing to the rail because of seasickness. But he soon got his sea-legs and could endure a mild storm along with the best of them.

Wesley's ship was armed with thirty-eight guns, all of them thirty-two pounders.

"How accurate are they?" he asked.

"They're good for well over a mile," replied a gunner.

Having settled into the routine of ship life, Samuel opened his notebook and began the poem that he had dreamed about during the last year or two. And whenever the captain dropped anchor at a port, he had a letter ready to mail to Susanna.

In one letter he wrote, "The Irish Sea is rough. Not only does the ship roll, but it also stands on one end and then the other. Our plates sometimes slide off the tables. But I'm getting used to the sea. We had a storm yesterday and I managed to stay away from the rail. This week I've started my new poem. It's titled *The Life of Our Blessed Lord Jesus Christ.* It will contain about ten thousand lines. These will be divided into ten sections, and then all of them will be published in one volume. If all goes well, I'll dedicate it to her Most Sacred Majesty, Queen Mary II."

Samuel enjoyed life at sea. He wrote letters for the men, preached, taught classes, counseled. And when Jim fell from a yardarm and was killed, he preached his funeral and said the last words as the canvas-wrapped body was slipped into the sea. But he could not keep his mind away from Susanna. Finally the tension became so unbearable he wrote to the Bishop of London and informed him that he would like to be a curate—especially if he could find a position in the London area.

Back at home, Susanna missed Samuel. During the

first month of his absence she counted the days; but within a few months she was counting the hours—and then the minutes. She passed the time by helping her father with his visitation, going on long walks—and reading. She loved theology and even studied the writings of the Early Church leaders.

Toward the end of spring, Elizabeth came rushing over to the Annesley home. Her face was radiant. "Guess what?" she exclaimed. "John has paid his most pressing debts! And that means he no longer has to wear a disguise and be afraid of his own shadow." She took Susanna's arm. "Have you heard when Sam will be moving back to London?"

"No news yet. But the Bishop is trying to get him a curacy."

"When you write, tell him that John is all excited about the magazine he's going to publish. And tell him John expects him to do a lot of the writing."

As the sisters were visiting, Dr. Annesley stepped into the room. "Another of God's laws has been proven to be true," he announced with conviction.

"And which one is that?" asked Elizabeth.

"The law of sowing and reaping. Brother Paul wrote: 'Be not deceived; God is not mocked; for whatsoever a man soweth, that shall he also reap' (Galatians 6:7)."

Susanna slanted her eyes. "And how has it been proven true?"

"It was proven with Judge Jeffreys. Remember how he slaughtered the people after the Monmouth Rebellion?"

"Yes, I remember," said Susanna. "He bragged that he had hanged more people than all the English judges put together since the days of William the Conqueror."

"This is what happened," continued Annesley.

"After James II escaped, Jeffreys disguised himself and boarded ship. His plan was to escape to the Continent. But while his ship was in an English port, he was so overcome by his thirst for alcohol he went on shore. There, as he was drinking at the bar of the Red Cow, he was arrested and dragged off to the Tower. He pled guilty; but he tried to blame his crimes on King James. While he was in the Tower he was so hated by other prisoners the officers kept him under guard for his own protection.

"Sooner or later Jeffreys would have been beheaded. But last week he died of stomach ulcers. Many are saying he reaped what he sowed."

During the spring, along with three week-long illnesses, Susanna became deeply discourged. An entire month had crept by in which she had received only one letter from Samuel—and it contained only three paragraphs. Also, there were no positions for him in London. Feeling discouraged, Susanna made an appointment to see her father. The clock was booming ten when she knocked on his door.

Having summoned her inside, Annesley said, "I'm glad you're so punctual. Those who are prompt at appointments are on their way to success." He pointed to a chair.

Susanna noticed a map on his desk, and just beyond the map was a short section of straw, a long needle, and a pan of water.

"Sir, I'm deeply troubled," she began, speaking in a low voice. "Sam and I are going to be married. I'm confident that our coming marriage is in the will of the Lord. But, sir, I can't get any more specific directions. I pray and ask for directions, but all I receive from God is the old word: *Wait.*" Susanna dabbed at her eyes and blew her nose. "Tell me, what am I to do?" Before her father could answer, she continued, "I still remember the time I came to you when I was thirteen to talk about the church. You reminded me that I was born during the year the guards at the Tower were named Beefeaters, Rembrandt died, and Stradivari created his famous violin. I know God doesn't want me to become a Beefeater!" She managed a smile. "But what does He want me to become? I have only one life to live—and I want to know. When you were my age you knew God wanted you to become a minister. But, sir, when I pray, all I hear is: *Wait! Wait! Wait!*"

Dr. Annesley frowned. Then he touched his chin. After slowly moistening his lips, he said, "It's true that God spoke to me early in life. But God doesn't always do that. He has plans for each of his children. But He is not always specific—especially about the future. And there are reasons for that. One reason is that if we were to know too much about our future our lives could be ruined."

"What do you mean?"

"If in my youth I had known that I would some-day preach in the House of Commons, I would have been so elated I would have lost my humility. Likewise, if I had known that I would one day be put out on the street without a job, I could have become so discouraged I might have dropped out of school.

"The main thing to remember, Sukey, is that God loves you, that He has definite plans for you. When He says *wait*, He does so with purpose." Raising his voice a trifle, Annesley added, "You know you are a very fortunate girl."

Susanna lifted her head. "What do you mean, sir?"

"It isn't everyone who has two dozen brothers and sisters. Children in large families have certain advantages. In a way I envy you, for I was an only child. By having many brothers and sisters, you have learned how to shrug at defeat, how to get along with people, how to rejoice with others, and how to be thrifty.''

"You're right about learning to be thrifty, sir. The coat I'm wearing was worn by Elizabeth, Mary, Esther, Martha, Judith, and Ann. And it wasn't new when we got it. It's been repaired so often it doesn't even resemble the original version.'' She sighed and, shaking her head, added, ''It was my lot to be the youngest!''

Annesley laughed and patted her on both shoulders. ''You've carried the trials of being the baby of the family with remarkable understanding. I'm proud of you! But you're also fortunate in another way. You were born in one of the most interesting periods of all time. The plague swept over London in 1665, and then the next year we had the Great Fire and three years after the fire you came along. The whole world is changing. And you have been able to sit on the front seat. Current events, Sukey, and history are great schoolmasters.

"Many fail because of one mistake—the mistake that ruined Oliver Cromwell, a man I knew well. By noticing how he failed, you can avoid the mistake he made. And so, let's review a little history. After Good Queen Bess died in 1603, James VI of Scotland became James I of England. (He is the one who gave us the Authorized Version of the Bible). At his death in 1625, his son Charles was crowned Charles I. I was only five then, but I can still remember the way people talked about it.

"Like his father, Charles I was obsessed with the *divine right of kings.* His favorite scripture was Romans 13:1—'Let every soul be subject unto the higher powers. For there is no power but of God: the powers that be are ordained of God.' He believed that he had been appointed by God to rule; and that, therefore, he was always right. Always! And because of this, neither House of Parliament was called into session for eleven years. Charles ruled like a tyrant.

"In 1640 the Long Parliament was elected. It was dubbed with that name because it continued to sit until 1652, and was not dissolved until 1660—twenty years after it was elected. Oliver Cromwell was a member of that Parliament. This legislative body did some fine things: it stood up to King Charles, and it eliminated the Star Chamber—the committee used by Laud to torture, prosecute, and condemn Dissenters.

"But the Long Parliament was not united. Some were for the king; others were against him. Those who supported King Charles withdrew and became known as Cavaliers because of their dandified dress. (They sported feathers, elaborate wigs, long hair).

"Civil war erupted in 1642. The Cavaliers took one side and the Roundheads—those who stood for Parliament—took the other side. They were dubbed Roundheads because of the way they cut their hair."

Annesley paused. He pushed the needle inside a section of straw and carefully laid it in the water. Then he continued, "I was twenty-two at the time and was all excited. It seemed to me that England was on the very edge of a new era—an era in which God's righteousness would prevail. I was ready to give my life for the cause.

"And since Cromwell was a member of Parliament, and was for Parliament, I was for Cromwell. After all, the Bible says, 'In the multitude of counselors there is safety' (Proverbs 11:14).

"Oliver Cromwell was a military genius. But he forgot, 'Not by might, nor by power, but by my spirit saith the Lord of hosts' (Zech. 4:6). After the battles of Marston Moor (1644) and Naseby (1645), he was almost in control of England. Ah, but now Parliament, for whom he was fighting, stood in his way! He had denounced Charles for not heeding Parliament, and now he, too, did not want to heed Parliament. And so what did he do?

"He went to the General Council, and the Council debated as to whether Parliament should be dissolved—or *purged*. The vote was that it should be purged." Pausing for breath, Annesley twisted the needle in the water to the east/west position. Then, after it had resumed its north/south position, he continued:

"And so at seven o'clock in the morning of December 8, 1648, a date England should never forget, Colonel Pride took his place by the Army in front of the House of Commons. As members arrived, only the favored ones were allowed to enter. It was like the Day of Judgment! Those out of favor were told to go home, and those who didn't obey were arrested. Altogether, thirty-nine members—mostly Presbyterians—were arrested. The Thirty-nine members were locked in a tavern nicknamed *Hell*.

"Approximately eighty members retained their seats. This group has been named the Rump Parliament. It was named that because it was only a part of the whole. Eventually this fragment tried King Charles and ordered his execution.

"The whole affair, Sukey, was wrong. And sometimes when I think about it, I'm almost ashamed I'm an Englishman!

"Soon even the Rump was too much for Cromwell. The members took too long to pass bills, and sometimes they even opposed him. Eventually his patience snapped. Without even changing clothes, he motioned for a squadron of soldiers to follow, and strode from his home to the House of Commons.

There, like a tiger in the zoo waiting to be fed, he sat and listened. Then he leaped to his feet.

"He strode back and forth as he pointed at one and then another while he denounced them. He called them drunkards, unjust men, and names I don't want to repeat. It was a terrible moment. At one point he bellowed: 'Perhaps you think this is not parliamentary language. I confess it is not, neither are you to expect any such from me. It is not fit for you to sit as a Parliament any longer.' He then jabbed his finger at the Speaker and ordered his men to 'Fetch him down.' And this they did, pulling him by his robes.

"Following this, Cromwell assumed the title *Lord Protector of the Commonwealth of England, Scotland, and Ireland.* He ruled with a determined fist. Indeed, he was just as dictatorial as Charles I!"

"And did Cromwell rule without a parliament from then on?"

"Not quite! Cromwell was clever. He had another idea. He decided that there should be a new ruling body—no, he didn't want to call it a parliament—and that it should be formed by nominations. Churches and others were told to make nominations of 'divers persons fearing God.' Those who made the nominations were ordered to exclude lawyers and accountants! Within weeks a group of one hundred and forty men was chosen—"

"How did they vote on them?" asked Susanna.

"There were no votes! Cromwell was against that. Also, he and his friends reserved the right to approve or disapprove those nominated. Some called this body the 'Parliament-that-was-not-a-Parliament.' But it is best known as the '*Barebones Parliament*'!"

Susanna's eyes widened. "Barebones?" She pulled her handkerchief into a square knot. "You mean bones without flesh?"

"Yes, barebones! It was nicknamed that because the delegate who represented London was Praisegod Barebones. He was a leather merchant and an Anabaptist preacher. I knew him well—"

"But was that his real name?"

"Yes, that was his real name!"

Dr. Annesley twisted the needle in the water again, and again it settled in a north/south position. "The Barebones Parliament lasted less than five months," he continued. "Then Cromwell arranged for England to be ruled by a parliament of four hundred members. But—listen carefully. *That parliament was scheduled to meet only once in every three years — and then for a maximum stretch of only five months!*"

"And who ruled during the remaining thirty-one months?"

"Oliver Cromwell!"

"Wasn't he worse than Charles I?"

"As a dictator who craved power, yes."

Susanna shook her head. "I think Cromwell's story is terrible. He was out to defend Parliament, then he went to a Rump Parliament, then to a Barebones Parliament, then to a Parliament that was invisible for thirty-one months out of each three-year period. What happened to him?"

Dr. Annesley pointed to his newly-constructed compass. "Which way is the needle pointing?" he asked.

"North and south."

"Correct. Let's see if we can change that." He slowly moved the lodestone around the magnetized needle, As he did so the needle shifted.

"Explain that, Sukey."

"The needle is more attracted to the lodestone than to the north pole."

"Why?"

"Because the lodestone is closer."

"Correct! And this is what happens to most of us. We seek God's will for our lives, but even as we seek it our inward compass is deflected by our own desires. In the beginning, Cromwell was an honest man. But as he began to have success his personal desire for more and more success overwhelmed him.

"If Cromwell could have continued with the same spirit with which he started, England would be a different place. But that is hard to do. I know from personal experience.

"When the Puritans got into power they made fools of themselves. They invaded the churches, smashed the stained-glass windows, chopped up the altars, tore up the *Book of Common Prayer* and used its pages for unmentionable purposes, pried up the brass plates over the graves on the floors of the churches, hacked the statues to pieces, stabled horses in the cathedrals, and even pried out the eyes of the monument of Edward VI. As I watched them, I was almost ashamed that I was a Dissenter!

"Finally, Oliver Cromwell died in 1658. He was followed by his son, Richard. Richard favored me. He gave me the lectureship in St. Paul's. But he was a weak man, and by this time the masses wanted to return to a monarchy. And so Charles II was recalled in the spring of 1660. And you should have seen the way the people celebrated! They lit bonfires, danced in the streets, played games on Sunday—and got drunk."

Susanna shuddered. "Is Charles II still called the Defender of the Faith?"

"As king, it is his title." Dr. Annesley stood and began to pace around his study. "But he's also the most immoral king England ever endured."

"Vowing vengeance, Charles II ordered the deaths of many. For a while, I feared I might be hanged.

Indeed, an officer began to write out a warrant for my arrest; but before he signed it, he fell over dead.

"The only reason I wasn't hanged is because, as the king said, he'd become weary of hanging. But in 1662 His Majesty did a terrible thing—" Annesley cautiously opened the door, then peered out the window. "I don't want to be overheard," he explained. "Yes, he did a terrible thing. His Cavalier Parliament passed the *Act of Uniformity*. That bill stated that every minister had to be ordained by the Church of England and accept the *Book of Common Prayer*. It stated that anyone who served communion without Church of England ordination was subject to a fine of 100 pounds, and that if he continued to do so he would be imprisoned.

"And, perhaps to make the law more dramatic, we were all informed that the Act of Uniformity would take effect on St. Bartholomew's Day—August 24. That was an ominous date, for it was exactly ten years before that the Catholics in France had slaughtered ten thousand French Protestants!

"That was a terrible time for dissenting ministers. Your mother and I spent weeks in prayer as we sought the Lord's will. At the time I was vicar of St. Giles and had the lectureship at St. Paul's. Those positions brought me 800 pounds a year!" He raised his eyebrows. "But, Sukey, the Lord directed me to refuse ordination in the Church of England. So, along with two thousand other ministers—Baptists, Independents, and Presbyterians—I lost my pulpit. It was a hard blow.

"But as always, the Lord was good to your mother and me. After I lost my position at St. Giles, I established the congregation where I am now. Many of the parish followed me. Remember the candlemaker, Mr. Foe?"

"Of course. But I know his son, Daniel, better. Dan wants to be a writer."

"All of this demonstrates that we must seek God's will. Go into your closet and close the door. Get on your knees. Search your heart. And make sure you aren't deflecting your spiritual compass. Then when you've discovered God's will, follow it!"

As her father headed for the door, Susanna said, "Sir, I know you spread that map on your desk to use for an illustration—"

"That I did," he replied. Returning to his desk, he ran his palm affectionately over the map. "This is one of my treasures. It was drawn by Sir Christopher Wren, and he autographed it for me. Sir Christopher is the greatest architect now living, even though he started out as an astronomer.

"This map was his idea of how London should have been rebuilt after the fire of 1666. Since over four hundred acres had been destroyed, Wren felt that London could be rebuilt in such a way that it would be the most beautiful city in the world." Pointing with the end of his quill, he said, "Please notice the arrow-straight avenues he had in mind. Some of them would have been ninety feet wide! Ah, but the city fathers turned his plan down. And why? Because Wren's plans meant that many houses and buildings would have to be shifted a few yards. And now, because of their lack of vision, London remains a city filled with narrow, twisting, hard-to-find streets. Future generations will look back at those city fathers with scorn.

"And that's the way it is with a lot of people. Instead of being willing to yield their stubborn wills, they insist on having their own way. Spiritual giants are the ones who keep saying yes to God."

"Even though God says wait?"

"Yes, even though God says wait!"

Queen of the Rectory

Unexpectedly, a curacy opened in the London area.

"But do you think you can support a wife?" Annesley searched Samuel's face with suddenly fierce eyes. "Susanna is used to living well. Thirty pounds a year is a pittance. That's not enough for one!" He thoughtfully rubbed his chin. "And where will you live? There's no rectory."

"We'll find cheap lodging, sir." Samuel tried to keep his voice from trembling, but was not quite successful. "Also, I have an agreement with John Dunton to be a regular contributor to his new magazine."

Annesley frowned. "Are you sure he'll be able to pay you? He has one foot in debtor's prison."

"God will help us, sir. Susanna and I have prayed about it and we are certain our marriage is in God's will."

Annesley smiled. "If it is in God's will it'll work out fine. Remember she's my baby—and also my twenty-fifth child. You must take good care of her."

"I will, sir."

"One more thing," added Annesley as Wesley paused at the door of his study. "I know you can't afford a coach on thirty pounds a year, and so I'll lend you mine for a few days. You'll need it in order to assemble all the odds and ends that are required for housekeeping. Just let me know ahead of time."

After Susanna and Sam were married in early 1689, money was extremely tight. John Dunton's planned magazine had not yet appeared. But, Susanna shared in the excitement of listening to the plans for the forthcoming paper. It's title, it was agreed, would be the *Athenian Gazette*. Both John and Sam felt that it would be a world-molding paper, and Susanna was confident they were right.

The new parish was small, but exciting. The vicar was a pleasant man and several members of the parish were unusually kind to them. They brought in dishes, pictures, fruit—and a much-needed broom.

Finally Sam decided that it was time to borrow the coach and revisit some of the historic places in London. "I especially want to visit St. Giles," he said.

"And pay your respects to John Milton?" asked Susanna.

"How did you know?"

"You're both poets, aren't you?"

"That was mighty sweet of you, Susanna."

Samuel Wesley's eyes misted as he stood before the grave of John Milton on the left side of the church. Shaking his head, he murmured, "Sukey, John Milton was the greatest!"

"Even though he was a Dissenter?" teased Susanna.

"Yes, even though he was a Dissenter."

As they held hands, Susanna quoted the opening lines of Milton's poem, *Paradise Lost:*

> Of Man's first disobedience, and the fruit
> Of that forbidden tree whose mortal taste
> Brought death into the world. . . .

Kissing her soundly, Samuel exclaimed, "That was great. It's too bad Paul forbade women to preach."

"What was that?" Susanna glanced at him sharply.

"Oh, nothing."

"Have you been reading John Knox again?"

"Certainly not! And I promise that I'll never read him again—at least when you're around."

They both laughed.

As Sam and Susanna were looking around the church, a bent old man shuffled up to them. "And so you're Susanna!" he exclaimed. "I remember when your father was the vicar here. He showed a lot of courage when he refused to accept Anglican ordination and had to leave here. But the Lord has blessed him and that's why they call him the St. Paul of the Dissenters. A few weeks ago I found a copy of a letter he mailed to the parish on November 14, 1661. That was just a few months before he had to leave. You wait here and I'll get it."

While seated in a nearby pew, Susanna read the letter that had been printed on a fine piece of parchment. The well-thumbed document read:

> I never yet, that I remember, went through my parish, without some heartaching yearnings toward my charge, to think how many thousands here are posting to eternity, that will in a few years be in heaven or hell, and I know not so much to ask them wither they are going. While God continues me your watchman, I shall affectionately desire, and solicitously endeavor, to keep myself pure from the blood of all men; and that, not only for the saving of my own soul, by delivering my message, but that you may also be saved by entertaining it.

It continued on in this fashion and was signed, Samuel Annesley.

"I wish you had another copy," said Susanna. "This is great and I'd like to keep it."

"Take it home," replied the old man. "I've read it so many times I almost know it by heart."

The grave of John Fox was at the front of the building, just beneath the pulpit. "His book, *Fox's Book of Martyrs*, has done more to spread Protestantism throughout England than any book other than the Bible," said Samuel as he and Susanna paused in front of it. "I almost feel that I am standing on holy ground! Few people realize the great power that can be spread by a book."

"I'm glad you do," replied Susanna softly. Then as Samuel stood reverently before the grave she asked, "Do you know the story of how Fox was inspired at St. Paul's?"

Samuel shook his head.

"Then, sir, let's go to St. Paul's. I'll show you something that will inspire you for the rest of your life."

As the coach moved into the street, Susanna said to the coachman, "Take us to Whitehall." Then turning to Samuel, she added, "Father was going to bring me here, but he ran out of time. So now we can see the place together."

"And what place are you talking about?"

"The place where Charles I was executed."

"But why would you want to see that?"

"Because of a poem I read about the event."

After the coach had parked, an old man tottered up to them. "Would you like me to tell you the story?" he asked.

"That terrible event took place just over forty years ago," he said. "The date was January 30, 1649—and

I was there. Indeed, I was one of the guards! A large
platform had been built right beneath those windows.''
He pointed to a series of high windows with his cane.
''The platform was draped in black and it was surrounded by a guard mounted on horses. Some feared
a rescue attempt.

''The day was cold, and those in charge wanted to
complete the execution in the morning. But at the last
moment, someone remembered a forgotten detail.
That detail was that the instant Charles I lost his head,
his oldest son would become Charles II!

''To keep that from happening, a bill was rushed
through the House which said, 'no person whatever
should presume to declare Charles Stuart: (son of the
late Charles) commonly called the Prince of Wales,
or any other person to be king, or chief magistrate
of England and Ireland. . . .'

''Finally, at about two o'clock His Majesty stepped
out of the window onto the platform. Fearing he might
tremble because of the cold, he wore two shirts. Then,
after handing a letter which he had written for his son
to the chaplain, the King said, 'I go from a corrupt-
ible crown to an incorruptible crown.' Then, without
flinching, he knelt and laid his neck on the block.

''The moment the King's head was severed, a loud
groan, like the sound of an incoming tide, rose from
the people.

The poet, Andrew Marvell, was present. Later he
wrote a poem about the event. The first lines go:

> He nothing common did, or mean,
> Upon that memorable scene,
>   But with his keener eye
>   The axe's edge did try.

''His Majesty, King Charles I, was a martyr. He
taught a lesson all of us should remember—''

"And what was that?" asked Samuel as he fumbled for a tip.

Drawing himself to full height, and speaking like an archbishop at the wedding of a king, the guide said, "King Charles, God bless him, took advantage of his disadvantage!"

After Samuel had slipped a coin into the old man's waiting palm, he said, "Thank you, sir. I will remember that."

On the way to St. Paul's, Susanna asked, "How much did you give him?"

"A shilling."

"An entire shilling?"

"Yes, of course."

Susanna bit her tongue to keep from making comment. But inwardly she thought, *We get only 30 pounds a year, and that is equal to only 600 shillings — and that is less than two shillings a day.*

St. Paul's was so surrounded by debris, the coachman had difficulty in finding a place to park. Webb-like scaffolding clung to every section of the building. "Sir Christopher has determined that this will be his masterpiece," muttered Samuel.

Unable to enter the building, Samuel and Susanna stood near the main entrance. "And now let me tell you about John Fox," said Susanna. "During the reign of Henry VIII, Fox almost starved to death. In that condition, he came into St. Paul's, here, to rest and pray. While he was wondering what to do, for he was utterly penniless, a stranger sidled up to him and thrust some money into his hands. This stranger told him, 'Help is on the way.'"

"And was it?"

"It certainly was. Three days later, the Duchess of Richmond asked him to tutor the children of the Duke of Norfolk while the Duke was imprisoned in the Tower. In this way he supported himself until he was able to write his famous book.''

"And that means that we can count on Providence!'' exclaimed Samuel, a faraway look in his eyes.

While Susanna and Samuel were discussing the providence of God, a distinguished looking man strode over to them. "Interested in the cathedral?'' he asked.

Susanna studied him carefully for a brief second. Then she exclaimed, "I know you. You're Sir Christopher Wren! You've been in our home at Spital Square.''

Sir Christopher smiled. "Yes, your father is a friend of mine. I gave him an autographed copy of my plans for a new London.'' Then changing the subject, he asked, "How do you like the new building?''

"It will be a masterpiece,'' said Samuel.

"And do you know how it's being paid for?'' asked the architect.

"Through a tax on coal?'' said Susanna.

"That's right. Coal is a pretty dirty substance and yet it is contributing to what will be one of the finest cathedrals in all of Europe.'' Sir Christopher eagerly rubbed his hands together.

"I'm puzzled about one thing,'' said Susanna. "And that is, how are you going to keep the pillars and that gigantic dome from falling down?''

"Simple. We are following the eternal laws of God! I learned about them when I taught astronomy. Amos wrote about the plumb line, and prophet that he was, he knew its laws are unchanging. Plumb lines never lie! They were used on Solomon's Temple, and we're using them here on St. Paul's Cathedral.''

After that final statement, Sir Christopher stepped over to a wagon overflowing with lumber.

"And now where shall we go?'' asked Samuel.

"Pie Corner!''

"And why Pie Corner?" asked Samuel.

"Because that's where the Great Fire of 1666 that burned four-fifths of London reached its maximum."

"And what do you want to do there?"

"Meditate."

He studied her carefully. "Are you feeling all right?"

"Of course."

The coachman stopped at the famous spot and Susanna and Samuel stepped out. "This is where the Great Fire reached its maximum," said Susanna. "It started in the house of a baker by the name of Thomas Farriner. How it started, no one knows. It started between one and two in the morning. The fire raged from September second until the sixth. It reached its limits here. Tens of thousands were left homeless. And if Sir Christopher had had his way, the new London would be the most beautiful city in the world."

While on their way back to their lodgings, Samuel had a sudden question. "Are you going to start another Great Fire?"

"I hope so," replied Susanna. "But I hope that the fire I start—I mean we start—will not only burn all of London, but all of the United Kingdom as well. And then I hope that it spreads all over Europe, and then all over Asia, and then all over America, and Africa, and Australia, and all the islands in all the seas. Yes, and I hope it burns all over the world."

As he stared, Samuel exclaimed, "I didn't know that I had married a firebug!"

"Marriage, sir, has many surprises," she replied. "All my life I've been raised in a Christian home. But much that I have seen and read has not been Christian—"

"What do you mean?"

"Is it Christian for Catholics to burn Protestants,

and for Protestants to burn Catholics? Was it Christian for the Puritans to destroy Anglican houses of worship? Was it Christian to launch the Crusades whose sole purpose was to drive the Muslims out of Bible lands?''

"You sound like a Christian revolutionary!"

"I am. And, sir, you and I together must start a fire of truth that will sweep the world . . .''

"But there are only two of us."

"That doesn't matter. The Great Fire was probably started by only one person." As she spoke, the confidence in her voice kept becoming more and more firm. Then she wilted like a spring flower. "But, Sam, I have a difficulty. I can't find out what God wants me, Susanna Wesley, to do."

"Maybe your trouble is that you are expecting God to assign you to a big task. Maybe your compass is being deflected by personal ambition. . . . You know, Sukey, some of the truly great people are the ones who were faithful in doing simple things—"

"Like?"

"Like Mary, the mother of Jesus; St. Francis of Assisi—and even your father."

While gripping his hand with a tight squeeze, Susanna replied, "You may be right. Anyway, I'm going to keep praying for divine directions."

Samuel's face suddenly came alive with a new understanding. As he peered into Susanna's face, he said, "A little over 300 years ago Pope Boniface VIII decided he needed a painter to add decorations to one of the buildings in Rome. And so he sent out messengers to find the best painter in Europe. One messenger called on Giotto di Bondone. 'You have a great opportunity,' announced the man from Rome. 'Lend me some of your best paintings so that I can show them to the Pope.'

"Instead of selecting a painting, Giotto merely dipped a brush in some crimson paint and drew a circle. Swish, just like that. Handing it to the messenger, he said, 'Take that to the Pope.' He then turned to the wall frescoe he was painting and added an eye to a mule.

"The messenger scowled. 'But that's just a circle! Don't you realize that a commission from the Pope will make you both rich and famous? Lend me a masterpiece. I promise, we'll take good care of it.'

" 'The circle is enough,' replied Giotto.

"When the Pope saw the circle he frowned. Then he asked, 'Did Giotto use a compass?'

"No, he just drew it freehand. His brush just went swish—"

"The Pope pondered for a long time. He studied the circle from one angle and then another. Finally, he said, 'It is a remarkable circle. And it does take a lot of skill to produce a circle like that without a compass. I truly believe that Giotto is the right man. Summon him to Rome immediately!' "

Susanna smiled. "That's a good story," she said thoughtfully. "I'll remember it."

Mother

A few weeks after their trip to Pie Corner, Susanna got up from breakfast, went to the other end of the table, and put her arms around Samuel. "I've just learned a new equation," she whispered.

"Like Newton's equation about gravity?"

"It's not that complicated. But it's just as true."

"And what is it?"

"One plus one equals three!"

He studied her without understanding for a long moment. Then, just as the mantle clock was chiming seven, a smile of understanding dominated his face. "When's it due?" he asked.

"It's not an it! It's a *he*. And if you don't mind, sir, his name will be Samuel."

"Samuel? And why Samuel?"

"For many reasons. Your name is Samuel and Father's name is Samuel. And besides that, I've been thinking about Hannah and Elkanah, the parents of Samuel in the Bible."

Samuel laughed. "But you know you're going to

have a baby. Hannah prayed that she would have a baby.''

"True. But Hannah promised God that she would give her son to Him. And just as Hannah gave her son to the Lord, I—that is we—will give our children to the Lord. And it may be, Sam, that our children will help change the world!''

"You have a lot of faith.''

"Of course I have a lot of faith. Hannah's God is our God!'' She started clearing the table. Then she stopped. "Do you know why my father was named Samuel?''

"Tell me.''

"His mother was like Hannah. She wanted a child. Then my great-grandmother began to pray that God would give my mother a son. When my mother knew she was pregnant, my great-grandmother became seriously ill and died. But before she died, she said, 'If it's a boy, he should be named Samuel, *for I have asked him of the Lord.*' And from the very beginning, Father knew that he would become a minister. He went to Oxford when he was fifteen.''

"That's an inspiring story, Sukey; and I'm glad that you have faith that our children will change the world. But don't you have any faith that my books will do some changing? Listen to this. Here are some lines from my *Life of Christ.*'' From inside his Bible he took a sheet of paper and read:

> The Father's image He, as great, as bright,
> Clothed in the same insufferable light;
> More closely join'd, more intimately one
> With His great father, than the light and sun.
>   Equal in goodness and in might,
>   True God of God, and light of light.

"Oh, Samuel, that's equal to, or even better than John Milton. I'm so proud."

Samuel Wesley, Jr. was born in the Annesley home on February 10, 1690.

The *Athenian Gazette's* first issue came off the press a few weeks later, on March 17, 1691. Scheduled each Tuesday and Saturday, the penny paper became popular. Its purpose was indicated by the subtitle: *Athenian Gazette; or Casuisistical Mercury, all the Nice and Curious questions Proposed by the Ingenious.*

Soon Samuel was dipping his quill to write articles on such intriguing subjects as whether the soul is eternal or pre-existant from creation, whether every man has a good and bad angel attending him and why there are spots on the moon.

On a Sunday night after Junior was asleep, Susanna brought out a sheet of paper and laid it on the table. "Before our marriage," she said, "we agreed to compare our genealogies. Let's do that now. If my divine calling is to raise a strong family, I want to know what kind of blood will be flowing in their veins!"

Susanna and Samuel studied the charts.

"As you can see," commented Susanna, "I don't know too much about my relatives. But I do know that for many generations back they were fine, honorable people. Also, most of them were Christians, and most of them leaned toward Dissent. As you know, my grandfather on my father's side died when Father was only four. Father looked up his parents' names in his baptismal record in a church building dedicated to St. Mary. That record records: 'Samuell the Sonne of John Anslye, and Judith his Wife.'

"Father was baptized on March 27, 1620—the year the Pilgrims founded Plymouth Colony. Grandfather 'Anslye,' as he spelled it, was wealthy. And since Father was his only child, he inherited his estate. But

Genealogy: Samuel and Susanna Wesley

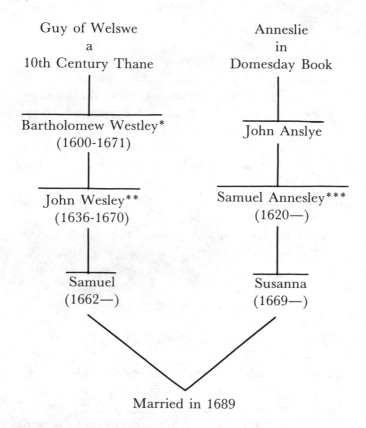

Guy of Welswe
a
10th Century Thane

Anneslie
in
Domesday Book

Bartholomew Westley*
(1600-1671)

John Anslye

John Wesley**
(1636-1670)

Samuel Annesley***
(1620—)

Samuel
(1662—)

Susanna
(1669—)

Married in 1689

*Dissenting minister. Lost his living due to Act of Uniformity on St. Bartholomew's Day, 1662.

**Sometimes he signed his name Westley.

***Samuel Annesley's first wife died after giving birth to her first child—a son. The second wife, mother of Susanna, had 24 children. She was the daughter of a John White.

when the two thousand ministers lost their pulpits due to the Act of Uniformity, Father was generous, and so he is no longer a rich man.

"Mother's father was John White, a Puritan lawyer and minister. He was also a member of Parliament and a distinguished author. Father visited his grave and copied his epitaph. I know it off by heart:

> Here lies a John, a burning, shining light,
> Whose Name, Life, Actions alike are White.

"Father's first wife was named Mary. She only had one child, my half brother, Samuel, Jr. Sam is now a businessman in India. I've heard that he's rich. Mary died in 1646. Father then married my mother in 1652."

Having made quick calculations, Samuel said, "Since you were your mother's twenty-fourth child, and since you were born on January 20, 1669, your mother must have had twenty-four children in less than seventeen years!" He shook his head. "How do you explain that?"

"Twins."

They both laughed.

"Will you do as well?"

"Perhaps. We already have another coming."

"Twins?"

"I don't know. But I think it will be a girl."

"Now, let me explain my family tree." said Samuel eagerly. Bending over the chart, he explained each point with his index finger.

"My father's father, that is my grandfather, was Bartholomew Wesley. He was a graduate of Oxford. Being plain spoken, he wasn't popular with his parishioners. Bartholomew was the father of ·my father, John Wesley, who was born in 1636.

"My father, John Wesley, married the daughter of John White, another outspoken man. And since John White refused to use the *Book of Common Prayer*, Archbishop Laud had him arrested—"

Susanna's eyes widened. "Did the Archbishop have his ears cut off?"

"No, he merely had him imprisoned. Then, when the Act of Uniformity was passed in 1662, both Grandfather Bartholomew and my father were put out of their pulpits because they refused to accept ordination from the Church of England.

"Since Grandfather Bartholomew Wesley had a background in medicine, he earned a living practicing medicine. Father, however, knew nothing about medicine, and so he could not do that. Those were hard times, for I was born just four months after he was driven from his pastorate. But the Lord took care of him. He went to the Presbyterians and Baptists and Independents. They kept him busy.

A few weeks after this conversation, Samuel returned to their lodgings in a vibrant mood. "Guess what?" he asked, beaming with enthusiasm.

"What?"

"The Marquis of Normandy has arranged for us to be appointed to South Ormsby—"

"And where is that?"

"It's up north in Lincolnshire about eight miles from Spilsby. I'll be ministering to about two hundred and fifty people. And, Sukey, I won't be just the curate. I'll be the vicar!"

"And how much is the living?"

"My salary is 50 pounds a year, and that includes a rectory to live in. Being out in the country, we'll have room for the children and a lot of quiet for my writing."

Susanna shared Samuel's enthusiasm even though she knew Lincolnshire was a backward place. Henry VIII had dubbed it "one of the most brute and beastly of the whole realm."

Sorrow

Susanna's eyes overflowed as she assumed her seat in the carriage and stretched out her arms for baby Samuel. South Ormsby was a little over one hundred miles to the north, and never had she been such a long distance from home. She might never see her father or the rest of her family again.

Soon the coachman flicked his whip. The four to five day journey was extremely hazardous. The roads were poor. The mud was deep. And there were reports that highwaymen lurked ahead. "What will we do if a bandit stops us?" asked Susanna.

"The Lord will take care of us," assured Samuel. He patted her on the shoulder. "And we don't have much to steal, except my books. Maybe a Greek New Testament would do a bandit a lot of good!"

Susanna was expecting her new baby any day. "What will we name it?" she asked.

"If it's a girl—and it will be—her name should be Susanna," said Samuel. "Yes, she should be named after the queen of the rectory—and that, my love, is exactly what you are!"

"That's very thoughtful of you," replied Susanna.

The roads were rough. On three occasions they had to stop and wait for Susanna's stomach to settle. She worried about the baby that was almost due and she worried about the child in her arms. Samuel, Jr. was vigorous enough. He had cut three teeth. But he had not uttered a single word. Not even "mama."

"I hope his mind's all right," said Susanna after spending an hour trying to get him to speak.

"Maybe he'll talk when he has a brother or sister," suggested Samuel.

Susanna had heard of the *wolds* in Lincolnshire and now on the fifth day of their trip as they drove through them she fell in love with their rhythmic appearance. The wolds—small cone-shaped hills—reminded her of buns crowded together in a baker's window.

Soon their carriage was creeping by the spacious lawns of the Marquis of Normandy's mansion, a wide brick building with six sets of tall windows stretching across the first floor and another six across the second floor. The flat roof was faced with a series of miniature brick turrets like those of a castle.

"The Marquis is the one who arranged for our appointment," said Samuel, nodding at the imposing building. "Since I'll be his chaplain, we'll be visiting him in his home. I do hope that his home won't make you disappointed with the rectory."

"Don't worry about that, sir. As long as I have you, I'll be happy." Susanna gave him a tight squeeze.

The rectory was deplorable. But as Susanna looked through it, she tried to be optimistic. "We'll be alone," she said, "and there is a wide yard for the children!"

Samuel was more realistic. In a poem he described their home and location:

In a mean cot, composed of reeds and clay,
Wasting in sighs and the uncomfortable day;
Near where the inhospitable Humber roars,
Devouring by degrees, the neighboring shores.

The North Sea lapped at the shore less than a dozen miles away, and the "inhospitable" Humber River, several miles wide across its mouth, cut deep into the mainland some twenty miles to the north. The church was made of stone, had a square tower, twin chapels, and was peaked by three crosses. It was a satisfactory building, and Samuel was pleased.

Soon a desk was installed in the study and Samuel got busy with his articles for the *Athenian Gazette* and the final chapters in his long poem about Christ. Often when he wrote lines which he felt were unusually good, he read them to Susanna. Once he said, "I'm doing the Transfiguration. What do you think of this?" He then read:

To Tabor's mount He beckon'd from the sky,
Two glorious saints who reign'd enthroned on high;
Moses, the leader of God's chosen band.

"You're doing well," she replied. "I hope your poem stirs the world!"

The baby was born soon after the move. As Samuel predicted, it was a girl. She was christened Susanna. Other babies followed in rapid succession.

Emilia made her appearance in January, 1692. Little Susanna became seriously ill in the winter of '93. Night after night Susanna sat up with her. But they lost the battle. Little Susanna died that spring. Emilia was now cutting teeth—and talking. Her first word was "mama."

But Samuel, Jr. remained as silent as a doorknob. His hearing seemed normal, and his loud crying proved that his vocal chords were healthy.

"Maybe Emilia will teach him to talk," suggested Samuel.

Susanna dabbed at her eyes. "If he would say just one word I would be happy." But the silence continued. Susanna held him by the fireplace and prayed for him. There were no visible results.

During that year when little Susanna died, there was one bright spot. Samuel's long poem was completed and a few months later he eagerly opened the package that contained his author's copies. The book had been issued by Charles Harper. It contained 349 pages and there were sixty copper plates.

The moment Samuel laid the book down, Susanna opened it. Aloud she read the title page:

> The Life of Our Blessed Lord and Saviour
> Jesus Christ: An Heroic Poem. Dedicated
> to her most sacred Majesty; in Ten books.
> Attempted by Samuel Wesley.

Susanna inwardly smiled at the word *attempted.* Aloud she said, "Oh, Sam, it's wonderful, and I'm so proud of you!"

In 1694, twins, Annesley and Jedediah, snuggled into Susanna's arms. They both died the next year. The second Susanna was born in 1695.

Mary was born in 1696. In time, Mary was nicknamed Molly. With her cradled in his arms, Samuel stepped over to Susanna. "Look Sukey," he said, "Molly has the brightest eyes I've ever seen."

"Maybe God has a special purpose for her to accomplish," replied Susanna, getting up.

As the babies were being born—and buried—Samual's pen kept scratching out articles and poetry. He wrote quickly and with little revision. Sometimes he produced two hundred verses in a single day.

The Marquis of Normandy, a scholar, became a

warm friend of the Wesleys. Together, they discussed science, literature, the New World, the Bible. But then he moved and the Earl of Castleton took over his mansion. The earl was a proud man and his morals were typical of the high society of that time. He was not married to the woman who lived with him. Moreover, everyone knew it.

Just after lunch one day, an expensive carriage stopped at the rectory and the earl's mistress knocked at the door. "I've stopped by to see the vicar's wife," she said sweetly.

In time her visits became regular.

"I don't like this," grumbled Samuel after her fourth visit.

"But maybe I can help her," replied Susanna.

Samuel snorted. "I doubt it. She knows that it's wrong to live with a man to whom she's not married. And I'm afraid she's casting a shadow over my ministry. You know Paul said, 'Abstain from all appearance of evil' (I Thess. 5:22)."

"And, sir, what are you going to do about it?"

"I don't know."

Susanna walked across the room and then she returned. "I think there is something that you and I ought to pray about together," she said.

"And what is that?"

"Junior! He's nearly four and he hasn't uttered a word. He can walk and hear and run—and eat. But he won't say anything!" She wiped her eyes and blew her nose. "This morning while I was having my quiet time the Holy Spirit directed me to Matthew 18:19. There, I read the words of Jesus, 'Again I say unto you, That if two of you shall agree on earth as touching anything they shall ask, it shall be done for them of my Father which is in heaven.' "

"And what shall we be agreed on?" asked Samuel.

"That Junior will start speaking. If he would just say one word—one little word— I would be happy!"

As they rose from their knees, Susanna said, "Now we've agreed on that, and I'm going to believe that God will fulfill his word."

Samuel smiled and embraced her.

The next December, Queen Mary became a victim of smallpox. Thinking of others, she allowed all her servants who had not had the disease to stay away. Heartbroken, and in spite of the danger, King William lingered by her bedside. Mary struggled hard. But she lost her fight on December 28, 1694.

Queen Mary's death shocked all of England, especially members of the Church of England. William had left matters concerning the church in her hands, and she had done a good job. She was generous, compassionate, understanding.

In the midst of the national sorrow, Susanna continued to coax Junior to speak. Day after day, while holding him on her lap, she said, "Now say mama— ma-ma." She articulated the letters as distinctly as possible, and exaggerated the movement of her lips. But each time Junior either ignored the lesson, pushed his hand into his mother's mouth, or slipped onto the floor to play with Emilia.

Then on a spring day an uninvited tomcat moved into the rectory. The full-grown cat was completely black except for the tip of his tail and his right paw. These areas were spotlessly white. Friendliness was his motto. Loud purring was a specialty and he was generous with his meows, licks, friendly bites, and rubs. Likewise, he was an individualist. When feline fashion decreed tails down, his flagpoled up; and when fashion decreed tails up, his trailed behind.

"And what's his name?" asked Samuel as he blotted his signature with a bit of sand.

"Barnabas!"

"Barnabas?"

Samuel frowned. He searched Susanna's face. "And why did you name him Barnabas?"

"Barnabas means son of consolation! And that's what he is. The children love him."

The readership of the *Athenian Gazette* continued to expand. Soon it attracted well-known authors. Johnathan Swift, Dean of Saint Patrick's Cathedral, and later author of *Gulliver's Travels*, became a contributer; and so did Daniel Defoe—the former Daniel Foe—who had grown up with Susanna in London.

Intriguing questions demanding answers kept showing up on Samuel's desk. "Listen to this," said Samuel, facing Susanna across the supper table. "This man wants to know the exact day Adam fell! And this man wants to know the height of the Tower of Babel." Samuel shuffled through more letters and then held up another written on green stationary. "Listen! This lady wants to know if Peter and Paul used notes when they preached!"

Many of the questions were trivial. They and their answers provided entertainment, but that was about all. And then one afternoon just after the earl's mistress had taken a lot of Susanna's time, a pointed question came in. After reading it several times, Samuel went to Susanna. "Here's a question I have to answer," he said, "and I'm afraid my answer— one way or another—will disturb a lot of people. I need your opinion. Here's the question:

> I'm a chaplain in a certain family which is not as religious as I could wish it. I am forced to watch the women drinking, gambling, and so on. If I say anything I will lose my living. But I do not want to be condemned as a partaker of another

man's sins. I would like to know how far a chaplain
should go in taking care of the morals of the family
with which he lives, and who employ him. Your
answer may be of great use to many besides
myself.

Samuel eased himself into a chair across from
Susanna. "Well, Lady Solomon, how should I answer
that? And please remember the good earl and his
mistress read the *Athenian Gazette!*"

Susanna bit her lip. "I-I really don't know. Why
don't you tell him to seek directions from the Lord?"

"And thus escape a direct answer?" asked Samuel,
his voice rising. As the subject was discussed, Junior
brought Barnabas into the room and sat with him in
the center of the floor.

Samuel thumped the letter on his knee. "The problem is touchy because far too many know about our
problem here in South Ormsby."

"You mean the earl's mistress?"

Samuel nodded. "Sukey, I must deal with that
problem or the Lord will hold me accountable!"

In the silence that followed, Emilia brought out
some doll clothes and began to dress Barnabas. She
fitted him with a shirt, tied a bonnet on his head, and
tried to put pants on his other end. But since there
was no hole for his tail, she had a problem.

Feeling a twinge of alarm, Susanna said, "You
know, sir, we'll have to be a little tactful. Our living
depends on the earl's generosity."

Samuel's eyes snapped with a new intensity. "You
mean you'd compromise truth for material things?"
he demanded, a scowl dominating his face.

"Not at all. But Jesus said, 'Be wise as serpents,
and harmless as doves' (Matthew 10:16)."

"And Shakespeare said, 'The better part of valor
is discretion.' But Paul means more to me than

Shakespeare, and he said, 'Touch not the unclean thing' (II Cor. 6:17).'' With that, Samuel picked up the disturbing question and strode out of the room. Soon, he was vigorously scratching out an answer.

With a chuckle, he wrote: "The pulpit is the most proper, and sometimes the only place to convince strangers of their faults. But private areas are convenient for friends and familiars.''

The day after Samuel had mailed his manuscript to London, he was finishing his breakfast when the earl's carriage stopped at the front door.

"It's the earl's mistress," said Susanna, excusing herself and going to the door.

"Let me take care of this," put in Samuel, reaching the door ahead of her.

"The earl's gone, and I thought I could spend a couple of hours with you," said the woman.

Samuel's quick eyes noticed her finery. She was wearing a huge black hat topped with green feathers, a daringly low-cut dress. Several of her fingers sparkled with pea-sized diamonds.

"I'm afraid, Miss, that you'll have to stop your visits to the rectory," said Samuel. "I'm here to preach righteousness. You're living in sin!''

As Susanna shuddered, the woman's mouth fell open. Then her cheeks flamed. As she retreated toward her carriage, she shouted over her shoulder, "The earl has a lot of power in these parts. You'll regret what you've said!''

After the carriage had disappeared, Susanna almost collapsed into the nearest chair. "Did you have to be so blunt?'' she asked.

I'm afraid so.''

"But, sir—''

"Truth is truth.''

"And what will we do if—''

"God will provide." Samuel was as unruffled as a lamppost.

The earl's unhappiness with the Wesleys was felt immediately. Both he and his servants stayed away from services and rumors began to spread that the Wesleys would soon be moving.

Discouraged, Susanna spent more time in prayer. It seemed that her whole world was falling apart. At one time she felt certain that her purpose in life was to raise and educate a large family—and that perhaps some of her sons would help change the world. But it seemed that this was not to be. Of her seven children, three were dead—and Samuel, Jr. had not uttered a word. Now they were about to lose their living at South Ormsby; and besides that she had learned that her father was seriously ill.

Could it be that God was remembering some sin in her life, and that He had forsaken her? Quickly, she reviewed her past. She thought of her doubts, flashes of temper, times of impatience—and pride. Yes, she had been proud! She was proud of her father, her quick mind, the many books she had read—and even her good looks. But soon she remebered how she had confessed her sins of pride, temper, impatience, and doubts to the Lord. Moreover, she knew that her sins—all of them—had been forgiven. Deep inside she knew that her failures were not the trouble. What, then, was it?

She opened her Bible and reread the carefully marked promise of Jesus, *"Again I say unto you, That if two of you shall agree on earth as touching any thing that they shall ask, It shall be done for them of my Father which is in heaven."* In despair she got on her knees, confessed all the sins she could remember, and searched her heart again. Then she turned to Matthew 7:7 and lingered on the words, "Ask, and it shall be given you; seek, and ye shall find; knock and it shall be opened unto you."

After wiping her eyes and washing her face, Susanna went to the kitchen.

Unhappiness in the parish continued. Those members who did not stay away from services often left without shaking hands with either Susanna or Samuel. And during her shopping hours at the market, Susanna continued to notice a deepening unrest among the people. Invitations to go out for meals gradually stopped.

"The fact that we are no longer useful in South Ormsby is as evident as the face of the moon," complained Samuel.

Worried, and with a new baby on the way, Susanna was forced to remain in bed.

In the midst of these dark days, another great sorrow touched Susanna's life. Dr. Samuel Annesley worsened and died on December 31, 1696. He was seventy-seven. His last words were triumphant. Those near his bed heard him say, "Satisfied! Satisfied! O my dearest Jesus, I come!"

While mourning over her father's death, Susanna received a copy of his will. As she read it, a new ache formed in her heart. She and her father had been close. He had entrusted her with the family papers. But now it seemed that she had been disinherited. How could it be true? The fourth paragraph of the document was pointed:

> "My just debts being paid, I give to each of my children one shilling, and all the rest to be equally divided between my son Benjamin Annesley, my daughter Judith Annesley, and my daughter Ann Annesley, whom I make my executors of my last Will and Testament."

Numbed by the blow, Susanna closed the door of
her bedroom, and kneeling by a chair, sought peace
from the Lord. Then, her cheeks streaked with tears,
she washed her face, combed her hair, and went
downstairs to see what the children were doing.

Emilia was playing with a handful of clothespins,
Susanna was combing Mary's hair, but Junior was
nowhere to be seen. She searched through the base-
ment, in the woodshed, and under the beds. Then
she opened all the closets. In desperation, she shouted,
"Junior! Junior! Junior!"

Finally a little boy's voice which she had never
heard answered, "Here I am, Mother."

Following the sound, Susanna peered under the
table. And there she saw Junior. His face was streaked
with jam and Barnabas was in his arms. And from
that time on Junior had a lot to say—and ask. His
favorite question was *Why?*

During the next week Susanna taught him to repeat the Lord's Prayer.

On February 11, the day after Samuel, Jr. was five, Susanna called him into her room. She said, "As I told you yesterday, you will learn to read today."

Then, speaking slowly and distinctly, she repeated the alphabet, and explained how to pronounce each letter. By noon he could repeat all twenty-six letters. Later, after lunch, and on the same day, she went over the entire lesson with him. He recited the alphabet perfectly.

On the following day, she opened the Bible to Genesis 1:1 and held it up to him. His task was to name each letter in the opening sentence which begins: I-n t-h-e b-e-g-i-n-n-i-n-g G-o-d c-r-e-a-t-e-d. They continued with each letter, word by word. He completed the lesson by noon, and again she went over the lesson with him in the afternoon.

Susanna knew that Junior was skilled at memorization, since he could repeat the Lord's Prayer. To make certain that he wasn't relying on memory, she had him read those same letters in other books. Within a few weeks, Samuel, Jr. could read the first ten verses of Genesis without hesitation; and by Whitsuntide (seven Sundays after Easter) he was reading the entire first chapter of Genesis.

Both Susanna and Samuel were amazed at his progress. Susanna set up school for Samuel, Jr. and began teaching him how to spell, how to write, and how to do adding and subtracting. This was the beginning of Susanna's school for her children.

Epworth

While shaking a long letter from the bishop, Samuel Wesley radiated with a happiness Susanna had never witnessed before. "Look at this!" he exclaimed. "God has proved His word. You are now looking at the new vicar of St. Andrew's Parish in Epworth."

"What do you mean?"

"This is our new appointment. Epworth is a wonderful place, and our living will be 200 pounds a year. That is four times as much as we are now receiving. And besides, there is land for me to farm, and a nice rectory to live in."

"And when are we moving?"

"Next month! Here, take the letter and read it yourself."

From the bishop's letter, and through other research, Susanna learned that Epworth, some fifty miles northwest of South Ormsby, was a little town of two or three thousand—and that it was the capital of the Isle of Axholme. This "inland" island, formed by rivers and a canal, was in the heart of Lincolnshire.

Some of what she read about Lincolnshire, however, was not pleasant. From a dog-eared book, she learned that Henry, oldest son of James I, had visited this area to hunt stag. The island was smudged with swamps, marshes, shallow lakes. About sixty thousand acres were under water—some of it three feet deep.

Before the royal party arrived, nearly five hundred deer had been driven into a section of the marshes called Thorne Meer. Helpless, their necks just above the surface, the deer had no means of escape from the miniature navy of one hundred boats. As Prince Henry busied himself with slaughter, a Dutchman focused on something else.

"What would happen," reasoned the schemer from Holland, "if this lowland were drained and cut into farms?"

King James liked his ideas, and so a contract was signed. Cornelius Vermuyden, the Dutchman, was to drain the area at his own expense, and for payment was to receive one-third of the land. Another third was assigned to the Crown, and the final third was to be divided among the tenants.

Vermuyden sailed down the Trent on the east side of the island. The natives scowled and dubbed his boats, "A Navy of Tarshish." Violence followed. Boats were wrecked, wagons burned, and dykes cut. The sluice gates were opened, allowing water to overflow the banks of the river. The people were angered and they felt they had good reason. Vermuydem broke agreements. Also, he did not do a good job. Land that should have been dry was flooded, and large sections of land which should have been drained remained under water. In this atmosphere, intrigue surmounted intrigue.

Moreover, the people had long memories.

The more Susanna read, the more her heart ached. She learned that Lincolshire had been known as primitive country for a long time. More than half a century before, Henry VIII had been caustic. Lincolnshire, he fumed, is ''one of the most brute and beastly areas of the whole realm.''

The day before they were to leave South Ormsby, Susanna paid a farewell visit to the graves of her children in the church cemetery. Lifting her street-length skirt high, she paused at the little mound over the first Susanna, then she went to the resting place of the twins: Annesley and Jedediah.

With her four children about her and a fifth on the way, Susanna took her place in the carriage that was headed for Epworth. There was no single highway to be followed. Occasionally there was a remnant of an old Roman road and sections of military roads over which Cromwell's calvary had galloped. These

sections had to be fitted together like a puzzle and
Susanna kept fearing that they might get lost. Also,
there were no bridges. When they came to rivers, they
had to depend on ferries.

After several days of travel, Susanna stepped out
of the carriage, and, gathering her weary brood about
her, stepped into the rectory. In the language of her
day, it consisted of "five bais, built all of timber and
plaister, covered with straw thatche, the whole
building being contrived into three stories, and dis-
posed in seven chief rooms—a kitchinge, a hall, a
parlour, a butterie, and three large upper rooms, and
some others of common use; and also a little garden,
empailed betwine the stone wall and the south." In
addition there was "one barn of six baies, built all
of timber and clay walls covered with straw thatche,
with outshotts about it and the house therebye."

As Susanna and Samuel viewed their new home,
Samuel bent over and whispered in her ear, "God
is good! And just think, Sukey, in addition to all of
this we'll have 200 pounds coming in each year."

Altogether, there were three acres of land. As
Susanna's eyes took in this space, together with the
hemp-kiln and a dovecot for pigeons, she exclaimed,
"This is a wonderful place for our children! And,
Samuel, I want you to pray that I will always be a
good mother."

St. Andrews, the stone church at Epworth where
Samuel would preach, was not only the most beautiful
building in town, it was also an extremely old one.
"Goes back to the twelfth century," said the
housekeeper. "Let me show you around. The various
periods of British architecture can be seen here." As
she spoke, her brown eyes glistened with pride.

"The Early English period (A.D. 1189-1272) can
be seen in the chancel area. Look at that beautiful arch

and the table arcades.'' Then pointing to the windows
at the west end of the north aisle, she added, ''And
they got their place in the Decorated Period (A.D.
1272-1377).''

''And how about the Tower?'' asked Wesley. ''To
what period does that belong?''

''Oh, that belongs to the Perpendicular Period
(A.D. 1377-1574). These walls live with history. During Cromwell's time, the Puritans caused a lot of
havoc. They pried up the brass plates over the graves
in the floor and melted them for cannon. Also, they
tore down the great arch and replaced it with a much
smaller one.

''Before the Reformation, when the church was
Roman Catholic, there were two chapels over there.''
She waved her hand at a place where the organ stood.
''One was founded by the Marquis of Berkeley. He
left money to pay for a perpetual mass to be said for
his soul, and the souls of his close relatives.''

As the Wesleys turned to leave, the woman said,
''My name is Sally and I'm lookin' forward to a-
hearin' you preach next Sunday. Have heard good
reports about both of you. But if you'll excuse me,
I want to say one thing—'' She took a step closer and
lowered her voice.

After peering all around, Sally confided, ''People
on this island hate the king—whichever one he may
be. One's as bad as t'other. And so if you have Tory
inclinations it would be wise to go easy.''

Nodding diplomatically, Susanna said, ''Thank you
very much, and please remember us in prayer. We
both want to do the will of God.''

Soon Samuel was busy with his preaching, writing,
christenings, visitation. The attendance increased and
both he and Susanna were happy.

The new baby was born in 1697, soon after the

Wesleys moved into the rectory. "And what are you going to name her?" asked Samuel.

"Mehetabel."

"Mehetabel!" He studied her curiously. "And why Mehetabel?"

"It's a biblical name, and it means God benefits!"

Both of them laughed and Samuel patted Susanna on the shoulder.

Life for the Wesleys was going well. The entire edition of Samuel's poetic *Life of Christ* had been sold and he was asked to make revisions for a second printing. While he was in the process of revising the poem, the Poet Laureate, Nahum Tate, wrote a poem that exalted Samuel's book in the highest terms. And this poem was printed in the preface of the new edition!

"Those lines will sell hundreds of copies," boasted Samuel. "And look, Sukey, the greatest poet of England has called me, Samuel Wesley, me, the 'great bard!' That means he thinks I'm a great poet!" Holding the book to his heart, be paced around the room. "Oh, I wish John Milton were here!"

The high moments didn't last. Troubles attacked from almost every quarter. At first the 200 pounds income seemed a fortune. With that, plus the rectory and the income from books, Samuel was certain he could save money. Perhaps even make investments. But that was not to be.

Earnings from the *Athenian Gazette* stopped when the last issue was printed on June 14, 1697. Then, there were unexpected expenses. Since the "Epworth living" belonged to the Crown—Samuel had been assigned to this pulpit by Queen Mary—he was required to attach a *Broad Seal* to certain documents. This required money. Next, there was the *First-Fruits tax*. This tax was charged to clergymen who had been promoted. It demanded that a portion of the added income be paid to the government. Samuel's share was 28 pounds!

Likewise, there was the *John of Jerusalem* tax. Originally, this 3 pound tax had been paid because of an ancient agreement to the Priory of St. John of Jerusalem. But after Henry VIII closed the monastaries, this 3 pounds was paid to him, and then to his sucessors.

In addition to the John of Jerusalem tax there was another 3 pound tax for tithes.

These items, however, were just the tip of Samuel's financial difficulties. After moving to Epworth, the Wesleys found that their furniture was insufficient for either the family or the rectory. Since they had no money, and were already in debt, a friend asked his goldsmith, who also served as banker, to lend Samuel 100 pounds. With this loan they bought furniture and acquired tools for farming.

During their second year at Epworth, the barn fell down. The repairs cost 40 pounds. Samuel's mother was another financial responsibility. Penniless, she barely escaped debtor's prison. And although Samuel's brother, Matthew, was a wealthy surgeon, Samuel assumed the duty of sending her 10 pounds a year. But this was not the end of his obligations.

It was customary for parish officials to assign deserted children to people more fortunate. The assigned parents were obligated to house, clothe, and teach the children their trade. When a boy was assigned to the Wesleys, Samuel laughingly remarked that he would train him to become a poet!

Shortly after their move to Epworth, Susanna became concerned about Molly. "She doesn't seem to grow," she confided to Samuel.

"Give her time! Remember how long it took for Junior to speak?"

"I've been patient for months. When the other
children were her age they were twice as big." She
hesitated. Then she added, "One day when I picked
her up, I noticed a bruise at the base of her spine.
Do you suppose the nurse might have dropped her?"

"Oh, Sukey, I don't think so. Think of the good
things. Molly has the brightest eyes of anyone I've
ever seen."

The day after Emilia was five, Susanna called her
into her room. "Emilia, you're going to learn to read
today" she said. And Emilia did. Now Emilia could
join Samuel, Jr. in his daily lessons.

Although her health continued to worsen, Susanna
maintained her classes and gave birth to more
children. John, her tenth, was born on May 18, 1699,
and died a few days later. He was followed by
Benjamin who came in 1700 and who lived only a
short time. A pair of twins appeared on May 17, 1701.
Neither lived long enough to be named. Then Anne
was born in 1702. She was Susanna's fourteenth child.

All of these children had been born in twelve years.
Of the fourteen, only six remained alive.

Life for Susanna was hard. But she had learned to
make each moment count. Dr. Annesley had taught
the power of systematic methods. Susanna used that
power. Sustained rhythm became essential. Each day
was sliced into sections, and in each fragment she
worked at a specific task. In addition, she had become
more and more convinced about the power of prayer,
meditation, and the constant reading of God's Word.

Sam's debts worried Susanna. And she was concerned about his carelessness with money. It seemed,
that money had a way of slipping through his fingers.
Though there were problems, Susanna loved Samuel.
She was proud to address him as sir or master.

Likewise, she prayed every day that God would bless him and his work.

Susanna's shining dream remained. That dream was that God would enable her to so inspire her children that God could use them to help change the world. Every evening as she stooped over their beds, she prayed that God would guide each one. Moreover, she was convinced that He would do just that.

For a while things seemed to go well for Susanna. The children were absorbing knowledge. Samuel's poetry was progressing. His books were selling. People in the parish were being helped. Her health was improving. Her sky seemed clear. Then suddenly her world blew apart.

But even stranger than the unexpected blow that almost ruined her life was the fact that it struck at the conclusion of her most sacred hour—family worship.

Forsaken

Samuel stood facing Susanna. His face had become granite and his eyes gleamed with a fierceness she had never seen before. "Sukey," he demanded, "why didn't you say *amen* when I prayed for King William?"

"Because William is a usurper and has no right to the throne!" She spoke promptly without a blink.

Samuel glared. His lips whitened. When he sucked in his breath and doubled his hands into fists, Susanna cringed. Later she described the scene in a letter she sent to Lady Yarborough on March 7, 1702.

> He immediately kneeled down and imprecated divine Vengeance upon himself and all his posterity if ever he touched me or came into bed with me before I had begged God's pardon and his, for not saying Amen to the prayer for the k(in)g.[1]

Having sworn his vow, Samuel Wesley strode into his study, packed his saddlebags, and headed for the

outside door. He mounted his horse and galloped away.

The next year Samuel worked in other parishes. This kept him away from Epworth. And since a curate had already been employed at St. Andrews, the curate took charge of the preaching.

Living alone with the children was hard. Day after day Susanna tried to find a solution to the problem. After hours spent in prayer, she tried to convince herself that William of Orange was the rightful king. With William's geneaology before her, she studied his family tree more closely. Going back to Charles I, she followed his line. Yes, it was plain that William III, the Prince of Orange, was a direct descendent of Charles I. But it was as plain as the dovecot outside that this Stuart connection was through Mary, who was merely a *sister* of Charles II and James II. And this meant that William's claim to the throne was an *inferior* claim. No, it was impossible for her to believe that William III was the rightful king!

In Susanna's mind, and according to the diagram, Mary—daughter of James II—had been the lawful queen. Both she and Samuel were agreed on that. And now that Mary was dead, the legal queen should be the second daughter of James II, Anne. Again, both she and her husband were agreed on that.

But what was she to do? Days and weeks, and then months, slipped by. The real reason for Samuel's absence was not generally known. When questioned, Susanna always had the ready answer, "Samuel is convocation man in the diocese of Lincoln."

As Susanna sought a solution, the impossible took place. King William fell when his horse stumbled. He died a few days later on March 8, 1702. This meant that Anne, daughter of James II, was queen. Hours later, when Susanna heard the crowds singing, "God Save the Queen," she thought her problem had been solved. But Susanna was wrong.

True, the problem that had separated Samuel from his wife was no more. But Samuel had sworn an oath, and he was determined that he would not break it. Heartbroken, Susanna dated another letter March 15, 1702, and mailed it to her friend.

> He cannot be convinced he has done ill, nor does the present change in State [William's death] make any alteration to his mind; I am persuaded that nothing but an omnipotent power can move him and there I leave it. He is in London at Easter where he designs to try if he can get a Chaplain's place in a Man of War.[2]

Although Samuel promised that he would take care of his children, Susanna was worried. She remained firm in her belief that King William had been a usurper; but she did agree that she would obey the decision of two referees, *provided she could name one of them!* Samuel, however, refused to agree; and on Easter, April 5, he left for London.

Utterly wearied and desperate, Susanna appealed to Dr. George Hickes. Dr. Hickes had lost his position as Dean of Worcester Cathedral because he had refused to swear allegiance to King William III. In her letter, Susanna was frank.

> If I thought or could be persuaded I'm in error I would freely retract...and ask his pardon before the whole world. He accuses me of pride and obstinancy and insists upon my making satisfaction for the injury he believes I've done him. I dare not plead guilty an Indictment, but yet I hope however I may in other instances be (guilty), in this I'm pretty innocent.[3]

Hickes was sympathetic in his answer.[4] "Wherefore good Madam, stick to God and your conscience which are your best friends, whatever you may suffer for adhering to them."

Samuel was finally persuaded to return to Epworth. But he only remained two days. At the time he left, he was grim. "I will never return," he said. By now Susanna had had more experience with the Lord, and she vowed to herself that she would continue to pray until Samuel returned to Epworth and their problem was settled.

Eventually Sam did return and Susanna's happiness was restored. Then a fresh disaster descended. The new problem was outlined in a letter which Samuel mailed to Archbishop Sharpe on July 31, 1702.

> On the last of July, 1702, a fire broke out in my house, by some sparks which took hold of the thatch, and consumed about two-thirds of it before it could

be quenched. I was at the lower end of the town visiting a sick person, and went thence to R. Cogan's. As I was returning, they brought me the news. I got one of his horses, rode up, and heard, by the way, that my wife, children, and books were saved; for which God be praised, as well as for what He has taken. They were altogether in my study, and the fire under them. When it broke out, Mrs. Wesley got two of the children in her arms, and ran through the smoke and fire; but one of them was left in the hurry, till the other cried for her, when the neighbors ran in, and got her out through the fire, as they did my books, and most of my goods. . . .

"I shall go, by God's assistance, to take my tithe; and, when that is in, to rebuild my house, having, at last, crowded my family into what is left, and not missing many of my goods.

I humbly ask your Grace's pardon for this long, melancholy story, and leave to subscribe myself your Grace's ever obliged and most humble servant,

S. Wesley

The archbishop sympathized with the Wesleys and let it be known that they needed financial help. The response was generous. Many distinguished people sent them money to rebuild the rectory. Before the rebuilding could be done, the Wesleys were obliged to continue living in the remaining one-third of the house. Here, in spite of the charred timbers and stench of smoke, Samuel Wesley became once again a loving considerate person.

As the months slipped by, Susanna continued with teaching her children, and Samuel went on with his writing. One evening while in an unusually confident mood, Samuel said, "When I was in London, the Lord gave me a lesson in his goodness. Remember when I was almost attacked by that foul-mouthed redcoat in Smith's Coffeehouse?"

Susanna laughed. "Yes, Elizabeth told us about it. That was the time you sent the waiter over to his table and suggested that the man wash out his mouth for having blasphemed."

"Well, this time when I was in London I was going through St. James' Park when I met that gentleman. He walked up to me and said, 'Remember me?' 'No,' I replied, 'I don't.' He then took a step closer and said, 'The last time we met was in Smith's Coffeehouse.'

"The old story rushed back to me. For a moment I was afraid he would beat me up. Do you know what happened?"

"I have no idea."

"He took my hand in his and said, 'I want to thank you. Since that time I have not said a single thing that would be offensive to the Divine Majesty.' "

The next year, on June 17, 1703, Susanna gave birth to her fifteenth child. "And what are you going to name him?" asked Samuel.

A faint but distinct smile firmed on Susanna's tired lips. While Sam held her hand, she murmured, "His name is John Benjamin Wesley!"

"Why two names?" Samuel studied her curiously. "None of our other children have two names."

"Because he's taking the place of both John and Benjamin, our two little boys whom God has already summoned home. And also, Sam, because I'm convinced that he's going to be mightily used by the Lord. John means *Jehovah has been gracious*, and Benjamin means *son of the right hand*! I've prayed that he will live to hold high a candle in this dark world."

As Susanna and John Benjamin gained strength, the Wesley family settled into methodical routine. Samuel had just published a three-volume history of

the Old and New Testament in verse. He was now
wearing out pens on other projects.

Samuel's speed in composing verses never slowed,
nor did his diplomacy improve. When he and some
other preachers were invited to the home of an
unusually stingy man, he composed a poem on the
spot and quoted it aloud:

Behold a miracle! for 'tis no less
Than eating manna in the wilderness.
Here some have starved, where we have found relief,
And seen the wonders of a chine of beef.
Here chimneys smoke, which never smoked before;
And we have dined, where we shall dine no more.

After Wesley had quoted the final line and resumed
his seat, the host lowered the chill in the room by shaking his head and agreeing with the theme of the poem,
"No, gentlemen, we won't dine here again. It is *too*
expensive!"

Though stunted in physical growth, Molly continued as cheerful as ever. Her mind became unusually keen. The entire family took pride in her. "Molly
is unique," said Samuel.

In 1704 Susanna's oldest child, Samuel, Jr.,
celebrated his fourteenth birthday and went away to
school at Westminister. This was an ideal place
because his uncle, Matthew Wesley, lived in nearby
London. Even so, Susanna's heart went with him.
Each day she remembered his needs in prayer, and she
kept a constant stream of letters headed in his direction. The one dated August 4, is typical:

> Particularly I am concerned for you, who were,
> even before your birth, dedicated to the service of
> the sanctuary, that you may be an ornament of the
> Church of which you are a member, and be instru-
> mental (if God should spare your life) in bringing
> many souls to Heaven .

You have had great advantages of education; God
has entrusted you with many talents, such as health
. . . a good understanding, memory . . . ; and if any
one be misemployed or not improved, they will certainly one day rise up in judgment against you.
To God's merciful protection I commit you.

Susanna Wesley

On April 5, 1705, Queen Anne dissolved Parliament. This meant new elections. Lincolnshire
quivered with excitement. As Susanna listened to
reports and noticed anxious faces, she was worried.
At lunch one day she said to Samuel, "I hope we don't
have violence." Her anxiety was increased by the fact
that she was in the eighth month of her sixteenth
pregnancy.

"The contest here is between Sir John Thorold and
Mr. Dymoke on the Tory side, and Colonel Whichcott
on the Whig side," said Samuel. "I'm with the
Tories! After all, they stand for the queen and the
church."

"Sir, I hope you stay out of it," said Susanna
wistfully.

"I'll try. But it will be hard."

On May 8, Susanna gave birth to a son. At the
time, she was so weary she was unable to nurse it.
Providentially, however, a woman who lived near the
rectory offered help. "I'll care for him until you get
your strength back," she promised.

Profoundly grateful, Susanna smiled. "Thank you
very much," she said.

Queen Anne was against Dissenters. Resenting the
persecution of Dissenters during her reign, Daniel
Defoe wrote a sarcastic, tongue-in-cheek pamphlet
titled *The Shortest Way with Dissenters*. It suggested that
Queen Anne could solve the dissenting problem by
hanging all their preachers and exiling all the members

found in their worship services. The booklet created a sensation. The House of Commons decreed, "That this book, being full of false and scandalous reflections on Parliament, be burnt by the hands of the common hangman in New Palace Yard."

Queen Anne ordered Defoe's arrest, so he went into hiding.

After the *London Gazette* ran a notice offering 50 pounds to anyone who "could discover the said Daniel Defoe," he was located and clapped into Newgate. His sentence was a heavy fine and to remain imprisoned "during the queen's pleasure." In addition, he was scheduled to stand for three days in the pillory. On July 29 his neck and wrists were clamped into the wooden frame in front of the Royal Exchange. The next day he was humiliated near the Conduit on Cheapside; and on the following day he endured the three-holed affair at the Temple Bar.

The masses sympathized with Defoe. Thousands swarmed about him at each pillory and decorated it with garlands of flowers. Defoe, himself, had carefully prepared for the event by writing the *Hymn of the Pillory*. The document sold briskly to the crowds swarming about him. Thus he enjoyed the last laugh and earned a tidy sum.

This affair, and others, had so stirred England that in some places members of the Church of England and Dissenters treated one another as enemies.

Fearing serious trouble would break out during the election, Samuel agreed to be neutral. But when office-seekers sided with the Dissenters and denounced the High Church, Samuel was infuriated.

"I will vote for the Tories!" he said.

Samuel's statement exasperated the Whigs. His own members even shook their fists at him on the steps of the church. Many denounced him as a "rascal and scoundrel."

Susanna was alarmed. When Samuel announced that he was going to Lincoln on May 29, the day before the election, she was gripped by sudden fear. This meant that she would be alone with the children on the day the voting began, and her unnamed son was less than three weeks old.

What would she do if she were attacked?

While Sam was in the courtyard of Lincoln Castle, a clergyman friend approached. "Sam, you'd better be careful," he warned. "I just passed a group of about twenty men. I heard one of them say that they were going to squeeze your guts out."

Fearing for his life, Samuel fled to Gainsborough. This may have saved him, for while he was gone a mob descended on the rectory. Samuel described what happened in a letter to Archbishop Sharpe:

> A great part of the night our isle people kept drumming, shouting, and firing pistols and guns under the windows where my wife lay, who had been brought to bed not three weeks before. I had put the child to nurse over against my own house; the noise kept his nurse waking until one or two in the morning. Then they let off; and the nurse being heavy to sleep, overlaid the child. She waked, and finding it dead, ran with it to my house almost distracted, and calling my servants, threw it into their arms. They as wise as she, ran up with it to my wife, and, before she was well awake, threw it cold and dead into hers. She composed herself as well as she could, and that day got it buried.

Having to bury her son without Samuel being there was extremely hard. But feeling that it was her duty in life to hold her candle high, Susanna managed with a minimum of trouble. By the time Samuel returned home, she had managed to get hold of herself. Indeed, she was so serene, Samuel was amazed. In the letter to Archbishop Sharpe he added the incredible line: *"All this, thank God, does not in the least sink my wife's spirits."*

The mob, however, was not satisfied. Upon Samuel's return, they beat drums, fired guns, and made as much noise as possible until midnight. Then on Friday evening, while Samuel and Susanna listened, the crowds shouted to their children in the yard, "O ye devils! we will come and turn ye all out of doors a-begging shortly."

At first Susanna was disturbed, but that night retreating into her fortress of faith, she put out the candle and was soon asleep.

Notes

1. Newton, John, *Susanna Wesley*, (Epworth Press, 1968), p. 89.
2. Ibid. p. 90
3. Ibid. p. 91
4. Ibid. p. 92

Prison

Susanna's world continued to crumble. Of her sixteen children, nine were already dead.

In addition to the constant problems of life and death, Susanna lived in fear that Samuel would be imprisoned for debt. Each rap at the door quickened her pulse. She had done everything possible to conserve money. It was wasted effort. Then, following the Duke of Marlborough's stunning victory at Blindheim near the city of Ulm on the Danube, Susanna saw a dim light at the end of the tunnel.

At the time of the death of the Spanish king, Charles II, Louis XIV decided that his opportunity had come to annex Spain and its entire empire. Alarmed, England, Prussia, Austria, the Netherlands, and much of the Holy Roman Empire, formed the Grand Alliance in order to stop the French and Bavarians.

Marlborough's victory was the turning point of the war, and the Duke of Marlborough became England's celebrated hero. Indeed, Queen Anne ordered the magnificent Palace of Blenheim built and presented to him as part of his reward.

Inspired by Marlborough, Sam wrote a 506 line poem in his honor. This poem inspired the duke to appoint Samuel chaplain of Colonel Lepelle's regiment.

"God is answering prayer!" exulted Samuel. "With this additional income, we'll be able to pay all our debts. You can buy some new clothes."

"The children need new clothes more than I do," put in Susanna. "The girls are almost in rags."

That wasn't the end of Samuel's blessings. A nobleman summoned him to London and started procedures that could end in his receiving a *prebend*—an endowment income—from one of the cathedrals.

Also, his field of flax was ripening, and it seemed that it would soon be ready to sell.

Alas, these near-blessings, all of them, turned sour. Politicians whom Wesley had offended used their influence to cancel his chaplaincy. Next, through their contacts in London, they ended his chances of receiving income from the cathedral. Shoulders slumped, eyes lackluster, Samuel turned to Susanna, "The Lord gave, and the Lord hath taken away," he murmured.

"Blessed be the name of the Lord" (Job 1:21), finished Susanna.

That evening, attracted by a red glow, Susanna went outside and discovered that all their flax was on fire. As she watched, Samuel put his arm around her. "I was counting on that crop to pay some debts," he murmured.

After breakfast, Wesley put on his robe and donned his wig. "Have a christening over at the church," he explained. "I'll see you at lunch."

As Susanna watched him disappear, she had an uncanny feeling that more trouble was ahead. She was right. Immediately after the ceremony, a former servant stepped up to Samuel. "You're under arrest," he said.

"And for what?"

"Debt"

"And to whom?"

"Mr. Pinder."

"Yes, I do owe him money. But it's less than 30 pounds. Give me time. I have furniture and cattle that can be sold."

"We don't have time for that."

"What can I do?"

"Pay the entire amount, or go to prison."

"Let me tell my wife goodbye."

"There ain't time."

Samuel was led away.

When Susanna learned what had happened, she went to her room, sank to her knees, and prayed. Then she began to plan a way out. Altogether, she had only ten shillings in cash. But a mere half a pound was not enough for a 30 pound debt. Then she remembered her rings. Yes, they would help! She wrapped them in a package and asked a servant to take them to Lincoln Castle.

The rings, she knew, would not pay the debt; but they would pay for Samuel's board and keep for a few days. In the meantime, she would sell a cow or two— even though she and the children depended on the milk for food.

Samuel Wesley took the affair in stride. On June 25, 1705, he wrote to Archbishop Sharpe:

> My Lord,—Now I'm at rest, for I have come to the haven where I have long expected to be . . . .I thank God my wife was pretty well recovered, and was (in church) some days before I was taken from her; and I hope she will be able to look to my family,

if they do not turn them out of doors, as they have often threatened to do. One of my biggest concerns was my being forced to leave my poor lambs in the midst of so many wolves. But the Great Shepherd is able to provide for them. *My wife bears it with that courage which becomes her, and which I expected from her.*

I do not despair of doing some good here, and it may be, I shall do more in this new parish than in my old one; for I have leave to read prayers every morning and afternoon in the prison, and to preach once a Sunday, which I have chosen to do in the afternoon . . . . I am getting acquainted with my fellow jail-birds as fast as I can, and I shall write to London next post to the Society for Propagating Christian Knowledge, who, I hope, will send me some books to distribute among them.

On the night following Samuel's arrest, Susanna heard the family dog barking and growling outside.

Terrified, she lit a candle and went from one room to another. Hurried inspection indicated that all the children were asleep and each door was securely locked. Satisfied, she returned to her room.

In the morning Susanna was gripped by a cold terror. The iron latch on the front door had been twisted off and three of their cows had been so severely stabbed they had gone dry. This meant there was no milk for the children. While considering what to do, the dog came whimpering over to her. One leg had been almost hacked off.

On Sunday morning Susanna dressed the children in their Sunday best. At breakfast, Emilia enquired about their father. "He's at Lincoln and won't be back for a while," she explained. "Our services this morning will be conducted by the curate. We must pray for him."

As Susanna sat in her customary pew, she battled with her emotions. Two-year-old John snuggled in her arms, three children sat on one side, and two on the other side. Only Samuel Jr., being away at school, was absent. Amidst the singing, Susanna was extremely conscious of the stares of those behind her and the question marks on the faces of those on either side.

Soon the curate, dressed in his new robe, stepped into the pulpit. His subject was the moral duty of Christians to pay their debts. As he preached he kept glancing at Susanna and her brood. His voice was cruel and his finger kept jabbing in her direction.

After the service, Susanna shook the curate's hand. This took effort; and she had to force herself to be pleasant. That afternoon she barely found enough food to feed her children.

Fire

While lingering in prison, Samuel Wesley had both cause and time to be discouraged. But he believed that "All things work together for good to them that love God." Even iron bars could not dampen his enthusiasm for the work of Christ.

During his third month of imprisonment, he concluded a letter to Archbishop Sharpe with a paragraph which no one but an optimist could have written:

> Most of my friends advise me to leave Epworth,
> if ever I should get from hence. I confess I am not
> of that mind, because I may yet do good there; and
> it is like a coward to desert my post because the
> enemy fire thick upon me. They have only wounded
> me yet, and, I believe, cannot kill me. I hope to be
> home at Christmas. God help my poor family!

Five days later, although still in prison, and still concerned about his family, Samuel Wesley addressed another letter to the archbishop. Having marked it "Lincoln Castle" and dating it, "Sept. 17, 1705," he began:

My Lord,—I am so full of God's mercies that neither my eyes nor my heart can hold them. When I came hither, my stock was but little above ten shillings, and my wife's at home scarce so much. She soon sent me her rings, because she had nothing else to relieve me with; but I returned them, and God soon provided for me. The most of those who have been my benefactors keep themselves concealed. But they are all known to Him who first put it into their hearts to show me so much kindness; and I beg your Grace to assist me to praise God for it, and to pray for His blessings on them.

Friends came to the aid of Samuel in his troubles. Susanna, also, was remembered. The Archbishop of York even came to see her.

"Tell me, Mrs. Wesley," he asked, "whether you ever really wanted bread."

"My Lord," she replied, "I will freely own to your grace that strictly speaking, I never did want bread. But then I had so much care to get it before it was ate, and to pay for it after, as has often made it very unpleasant to me. I think to have bread on such terms is the next degree of wretchedness to having not at all."

On the following morning the church official from York returned with a "handsome present."

After three or four months of imprisonment Sam was back at Epworth—and life continued as usual. On May 8, 1706, Susanna gave birth to her seventeenth child—a daughter whom they named Martha. Then a little over nineteen months later, she was confined again. This time the baby—a son—was two months early. At first he neither cried nor opened his eyes, and he wasn't much larger than a farmer's shoe.

Remembering the two sets of twins and other infants she had lost, Susanna wondered if this one

would live—especially since he seemed even more feeble than some who had died. Peering at him doubt-
fully, the midwife said, "Keep him wrapped in warm
wool for at least two months."

Susanna felt a special need to keep praying for this
new one who had made his appearance on December
18, 1707. It was a cold winter and there were drafts
in the house. Miraculously, he stayed alive. In
February he opened his eyes.

"And what are you going to name him?" asked
Samuel after his first most welcome cry.

"Charles."

"That isn't a biblical name. All the others—"

"Sir, that doesn't matter. His name is Charles!"

About this time, Samuel appeared at the rectory
with a heavy, expensive-looking book.

"And what is that?" asked Susanna.

"This is *Walton's Polyglott Bible.*" Samuel laid it on
the table and slowly leafed through it. "The Old and
New Testaments have been printed in both Greek and
Hebrew. In addition, other parts are printed in ad-
ditional languages. The first five books are in
Samaritan. Some of it is in Arabic, Syrian, Chaldean,
Persian—and even Ethiopian."

"It must have cost a fortune-"

"Yes, it did. But Sukey, I'm going to write a
Commentary on the Book of Job. It may take twenty to
twenty-five years. It will be my life's work. And,
Sukey, it will earn us a fortune. Future generations
will remember me as Samuel Wesley, author of the
Commentary on the Book of Job!"

Day after day, Samuel closed the door in his study
in order to keep his appointment with Job. He read
the text in other languages and filled page after page
with notes. "This commentary has to be the best,"
he said. But one morning as he emerged from his

study he held something different in his ink-stained fingers.

"While I was in prison, I kept thinking about the Cross," he said. "And this morning I had to forget Job for a while and work on a hymn. I've titled it *Behold the Saviour of Mankind.* Listen to the first verse.

> Behold the Saviour of mankind
> Nail'd to the shameful tree!
> How vast the love that Him inclined
> To bleed and die for thee!

"The Cross, Sukey, and the Resurrection are the great events in the history of mankind."

The clock had just passed the midnight hour on February 9, 1709, when twelve-year-old Hetty (Mehetabel) was awakened by the smell of fire and a shower of sparks. Terrified, she leaped out of bed to awaken the family. "Fire! Fire!" she shouted, as she pounded on her father's door.

Dressed in only a pullover gown and one stocking, Samuel seized his pants and ran to the room where his sick wife was sleeping with Emilia and Susanna. "Fire! Fire!" he repeated.

Startled from deep sleep, Susanna thought about the 20 pounds in gold and silver stored in her room. But with the flames pushing in, and being eight months along in her latest pregnancy, there was no time to look for it. Soon the entire family with the exception of six-year-old John was in the hallway. But the outside door was locked and the keys were above the stairway.

While shielding his face with his pants held high in his right hand, Samuel rushed up the steps, secured the keys, opened the door, and let the family out. "Where is Jackie?" cried Susanna.

Samuel had assumed that John was outside. But

where was he? As he pondered, he heard a tiny voice
in the upstairs nursery. Now that the door was open,
a northeast wind blew into the house fanning the
flames, and the steps were burning. Nonetheless,
Samuel tried three times to mount them. Each time
he was turned back. In desperation, he sank to his
knees in the flaming hall and gave the soul of his child
to God.

In the meantime, a nurse escaped with Charles in
her arms. She had just stepped out of the danger area
when a man confronted her. Having cursed, he
exclaimed, ''And so they burned their house again
for the second time.!''

While staring at the house bulging with fire,
Susanna was dominated by one determination. She
had to rescue John! ''I was not in condition to climb
windows,'' she wrote, ''neither could I get to the
garden door, but was driven back by the fury of the
flames.''

Having on nothing but a wrapping-gown, a pair
of shoes, and a loose gown, Susanna waded through
several yards of flame. But those growing tongues of
fire were too much. Unable to proceed, she prayed,
''Lord, help me save John,'' and tried again, and then
again. It was like stepping into the mouth of a furnace.

As this was going on below, John opened his eyes.
Seeing the light, he supposed it was time to get up.
After yawning, he called for someone to help him get
ready for breakfast. When no one responded, he
opened the door and was confronted by lapping
flames. After closing the door, he went to the window and scrambled up on a chest. At that moment
someone in the yard saw him.

''There he is! Get a ladder!'' called a man almost
beside himself with excitement.

''There isn't time!'' screamed another.

Then a stout man flattened himself on the wall. "Put a man on my shoulders," he shouted.

A tall, thin man ran over and positioned himself on the stout man's shoulders. By stretching he barely reached the window. Miraculously, he got hold of John and eased him to the ground. Moments later the roof fell in and lighted the Epworth sky with an inferno of sparks.

At first Samuel could not believe that little John was still alive. Indeed, he was not convinced until he had kissed him two or three times. Then he became alarmed about the whereabouts of Susanna. "Where's my wife?" he shouted.

Several pointed to her. She was standing in the crowd. But as Wesley remarked later, "When I came to her, her lips were black. I did not know her."

It was soon learned that almost all of Wesley's library had been destroyed; and included in this destruction were Dr. Annesley's private papers, Samuel's recent revision of his *Life of Christ*, and many other valuables. But Samuel was not overly concerned. Thankful that both John and his wife were alive, he turned to those about him and said, "Come, neighbors, let us kneel down; let us give thanks to God; He has given me all my eight children; let the house go; I am rich enough!"

The New Rectory

The day after the fire, Samuel searched the ruins. Everywhere he was faced with charred wood, scorched plaster, burned straw. Their clothes, beds, pewter, furniture, candles, books were all ruined. Fortunately, half of his barley had not been threshed and it remained in the barn. Also, there were pieces of lumber intact beneath the remains of the stairs. Otherwise, nothing of value seemed to remain.

But as Samuel searched further, he kicked up a lump of silver. This had been formed by the coins hidden in Susanna's room. In the garden he found a scorched leaf of his Polyglott Bible. Folding it carefully, he put it in his pocket. Then he went through the remains of his study. All he found was the sheet of paper on which he had scribbled his hymn about the Cross.

He would have stayed and searched longer, but he feared Susanna might need him. So he hurried to the home of the friend where they were staying.

"See what I found!" He waved the scorched sheet. "This is all that's left of my Polyglott Bible!"

"And from what section is it?" Susanna, who was resting after the ordeal of the fire, painfully forced herself to turn toward him.

"I don't know. Let me look." Samuel held the page to the light. Finally, he said, "There's only one line that's legible. Let me see. It says, '*Vade, vende omnia quae habes, et attolle crucem, et sequere me.*'

Susanna frowned. "And what does that mean?"

"It's Latin for, 'Go sell all that thou hast; and take up thy cross, and follow me.'"

"And what's on the other paper?"

"The hymn I titled, '*Behold the Saviour of Mankind.*' I was glad it survived, for I got the inspiration to write it while I was locked up in Lincoln Castle." He unfolded it and held it toward the window. "And all of it, Sukey, is here. I'll read you the fourth and sixth verses:

> Tis done! the precious ransom's paid;
>   "Receive My soul," He cries:
> See where He bows His sacred head!
>   He bows His head and dies!

> Thy loss our ruins did repair,
>   Death, by Thy death, is slain;
> Thou wilt at length exalt us where
>   Thou dost in glory reign.

"How do you like that?"

"Oh, Sam, it's great! I'm so proud. That and the single page from the Polyglott Bible were saved by a special act of Providence!"

"Yes, Sukey, Romans 8:28 is just as certain as up and down."

While Susanna stayed in bed, hoping not to

miscarry, Samuel was busy helping supervise the rebuilding of the rectory. Since this was in the midst of Queen Anne's reign when red brick was popular, new foundations were poured and red brick was laid. The new building, perhaps no larger than the old, was three stories high. There was a dining room, study, and parlor. The bedrooms were upstairs, and above them on the third floor was a spacious attic.

Since the children were scattered in various homes, Susanna was forced to interrupt their schooling. This was a trial. But as she awaited the new baby, she spent time reading, writing, planning—and seeking the Lord's will. The new baby made her appearance in March, 1709.

"And what's her name?" asked Samuel.

"Kezziah," replied Susanna.

"And why Kezziah?"

"After Job's fortunes were restored, he had three daughters. Kezziah was the second—"

"But why didn't you name her Jemima after the first daughter or Kerenhappuch after the third?"

"Because I like Kezziah!"

That spring, after Samuel had set out a sycamore tree in the churchyard, he went to the study in the rectory which was nearing completion. Soon there was a knock at the door and Susanna stepped in.

"Sir, you're more of a theologian than I am," she said. "I have a problem which you can solve."

Samuel smiled. "I'll do what I can."

"During the last fifteen years or so I've been convinced that my calling has been to raise a Christian family. And to do this I need every source of strength I can find. From my father and others, I've learned many sources of strength.

"Father taught me the power of method, of doing the same thing every day at the same time. And from

the Bible I've learned the power of prayer, and that
of studying the Bible. The promises are full of
strength. Also, I've learned the power of fasting. I
learned that from the statements of Jesus.

"But—" At this point she choked up and began
to wipe her eyes. "But there is a power that I think
all of us are missing—"

"And what is that?"

"Think, sir, of the power we could have if we really
knew that we were saved!"

"Oh, but Sukey, we can't know that! We can only
do the best we can, and hope. The hymn says, 'Doubtful and insecure of bliss, since death alone confirms
me His.'"

"Yes, I know, sir, that is what we believe. When
my sister Elizabeth was on her deathbed, she said,
'I have good ground to hope that when I die, through
Christ, I shall be blessed.' But, can't we be sure?"

Samuel shrugged. Then he scratched his ear. "I'm
afraid that you've asked a difficult question."

Susanna smiled. "When I was a girl my father
explained to me how long it took to develop the compass. Then he said that it takes just as long for the
hidden truths of the New Testament to be fully or even
partially understood. For example, think how long it
took for the world to relearn that the just shall live
by faith?" She paused to adjust the knot of hair at
the back of her head.

"Go on," encouraged Samuel.

"Well, as you may know, father and John Bunyan
were both born near Bedford. And even though
Bunyan was an Anabaptist, and father was eight years
older than Bunyan, father really admired him. As a
family we read his books. Father loved *Pilgrim's Progress.* He bought a copy of the first edition.

"Anyway, Father heard Bunyan preach and he was

impressed. Indeed, he wrote down a paragraph of his sermon and years later read it to me. I copied it, and here it is. Listen:

> One day as I was passing into the fields, still with some fears in my heart, suddenly this sentence fell into my soul, "Thy righteousness is in heaven"; and methought I saw with the eye of my soul, Jesus Christ at God's right hand. I saw, moreover, that it was not my good frame of heart that made my righteousness better, nor yet my bad frame that made my righteousness worse; for my righteousness was Jesus Christ Himself, the same yesterday, today, and forever. Now did my chains fall from my legs; I was loosed from my afflictions and irons. Oh, me thought, Christ! Christ! there was nothing but Christ before my eyes.

"Now, sir, what do you think of that?" Susanna riveted her eyes on his as she waited for an answer.

"I don't know," he replied slowly. "Bunyan at least proved that he believed what he taught. And it was because he refused to change his doctrine that he had to remain in prison." Samuel shook his head. "I often think of his court trials and his poverty and his blind daughter Mary. He was one of the great men of the century and his books are among the most influential books that have ever been written."

"But do you believe that he had a scriptural right to believe that he was really and truly saved and that there was no doubt about it?"

Wesley rubbed his forehead. After biting his lip, he said, "Really, Sukey, I don't know. Maybe the Lord used Bunyan to reveal that truth to the world."

Their conversation was interrupted by the clock. It was time to eat.

Susanna and the family moved into the rebuilt

rectory late in the winter of 1710. After viewing it, she said, "I like it very much. But Sam, we don't have enough furniture"

Samuel shrugged. "Maybe my book on Job will take care of that."

"And I also hope it earns enough to buy us some clothes," added one of the girls. "I've been dressed in rags long enough. I'd like to have at least one modest bustle!"

As soon as the family was settled, even though there was only half enough furniture, Susanna was prepared to start classes again. Thankful for what he had learned, John later wrote to his mother and asked her to outline the methods she used in raising and educating her children. In a letter dated July 24, 1732, Susanna replied:

> The children were always put into a regular method of living in such things as they were capable of, from their birth; as in dressing and undressing, changing their linen, etc. The first quarter commonly passed in sleep. After that they were, if possible, laid into their cradle awake, and rocked to sleep.
>
> When turned a year old (and some before) they were taught to fear the rod and to cry softly, by which means they escaped abundance of correction. The family usually lived in as much quietness as if there had not been a child among them.
>
> As soon as they were grown pretty strong they were confined to three meals a day. At dinner their little table and chairs were set by ours. If they wanted aught they whispered to the maid. Drinking or eating between meals was never allowed, unless in case of sickness. Nor were they suffered to go into the kitchen to ask anything of the servants when they were at meat: if it was known that they did so, they were

certainly beat, and the servants severely reprimanded.

At six o'clock, as soon as family prayer was over, they had their supper; at seven the maid washed them, and beginning at the youngest, she undressed them and got them to bed by eight, at which time she left them in their several rooms awake.

Susanna then went on to describe how and why she disciplined her children.

> In order to form the minds of children, the first thing to be done is to conquer their will. To inform the understanding is a work of time, and must. . .proceed by slow degrees. I call cruel, parents who permit their children to get habits which they know must be afterwards broken.

After many more observations on that subject, Susanna wrote about how she gave religious instructions to her little ones.

> Our children were taught as soon as they could speak the Lord's prayer, which they were made to say at rising and bedtime, to which, as they grew bigger, were added a short prayer for their parents . . . and some portion of Scripture as their memories could bear. They were very early made to distinguish the Sabbath from other days. They were taught to be still at family prayers, and to ask a blessing immediately after, which they used to do by signs, before they could kneel or speak.

> They were quickly made to understand they could have nothing they cried for, and instructed to speak handsomely for what they wanted. They were not suffered to ask even the lowest servant for aught without saying, "Pray give me such a thing."

Taking God's name in vain, cursing and swearing, profanity, obscenity, rude, ill-bred names, were never heard among them; nor were they ever permitted to call each other by their proper names without the addition of brother or sister.

There was no such thing as loud playing or talking. . .everyone was kept close to business for six hours of school.

One day Susanna was teaching a difficult rule of grammar, and Kezzy could not understand it. Patiently, Susanna went over it again and again. Then, noticing a shadow, she lifted her eyes and discovered that Samuel had been listening. Shaking his head, he commented, "I wonder at your patience, Sukey. You have told that child twenty times that same thing."

Susanna smiled. "If I had satisfied myself by mentioning it only nineteen times, I should have lost all my labor. It was the twentieth time that crowned it!"

Late one evening while tiptoeing through the
children's rooms when they were asleep, she was made
especially aware of their different talents. Kezzy had
been slow in learning the alphabet. (It had taken her
a day and a half!) But she had learned to read New
Testament Greek when she was eight. Both Charles
and Hetty loved poetry, and John was in love with
logic. Indeed, Samuel had once remarked that John
would not respond to the most urgent call of nature
unless he was assured of a logical reason to do so.

As Susanna lifted her candle to peer into each face,
she silently prayed for guidance to help that life count.
In time, she developed a method. Each day was
assigned for a conference. The date was inflexible.
Each child knew when it was coming. "On Monday,
I talk with Molly; on Tuesday, with Hetty; Wednesday, with Nancy; Thursday, with John; Friday, with
Patty; Saturday with Charles, and with Emily and
Sukey together on Sunday." And since Samuel, Jr.,
was away at school, she kept in contact with him
through regular correspondence.

Susanna was convinced that each child was equally
important; and she had an uncanny way of making
each one feel important. She remembered how her
father had made her feel important by reminding her
that she was born in the same year that Rembrandt
died and that Stradivari developed his famous violin.
In various subtle ways, she tried to do the same. Also,
she periodically asked each child to stand by the wall
while she recorded their heights, names, and the date.

Childhood diseases were constantly on the prowl,
and many invaded the rectory. Each child was taught
to swallow a prescribed medicine without murmur and
Susanna had little trouble in dosing them.

At that time many bizarre medicines were available.
It was alleged that malaria could be cured by wearing

chips from a hangman's tree. Washing the face only once a week and then drying it daily with a scarlet cloth was also considered helpful. A cure for a hearing loss was known by many. "Take a grey snaile, prick him, and put the water that comes from him into the eare and stop it with blackwool."

The children's teeth were a problem. At the time, *tooth drawers* wandered about hawking their services, offering to pull teeth. Each carried a dentist's "key" decorated by an assortment of teeth which had been "drawn." Patients were treated while seated on the nearest stump or other convenient elevation such as a house step.

While Samuel was in London in April, 1712, five of the children came down with smallpox. Susanna wrote him, "John bore his disease bravely like a man, and indeed a Christian, without any complaint."

Susanna did a good job. All recovered. None was afflicted with pitted faces, the usual badge of recovered victims of smallpox.

Our Society

Samuel Wesley's books and colorful life kept him before the public. On three occasions he was summoned to London to represent his diocese. Samuel enjoyed these extended trips—even though there was no expense account, and the wolf of poverty continued to snarl just outside his door.

A Mr. Inman had been employed to assist him as his curate while he was in London in 1710. Inman was a poor substitute. The people tired of his one theme: the necessity of paying one's debts. And since he did not bother with an evening service, Susanna began to conduct evening worship for her children. Soon the servants asked permission to attend. Then relatives of the servants showed up. In time, as many as two hundred people came.

These services were conducted in the rectory kitchen and quite frequently many people were turned away for lack of standing room. A typical service included the reading of prayers from the *Book of Common Prayer* and the singing of psalms. Also, on each occasion,

Susanna read a sermon which she had selected from her husband's library. The sermons came from books published by John Bunyan, Richard Baxter, and others.

Susanna never preached nor assumed the role of a minister. But her success and the fact that she drew larger crowds than the curate was too much for him. He sent a scathing letter to Samuel in London. Samuel agreed that Susanna should not be conducting such services, that her place was in the home—not in the pulpit. In reply to Samuel, Susanna wrote a long letter which has become a classic:

> As I am a woman, so I am also mistress of a large family. And though the superior charge of souls contained in it lies upon you, as head of the family, and as their minister; yet in your absence I cannot but look upon every soul you leave under my care as a talent committed to me.
>
> As for your proposal of letting some other person read. Alas! you do not consider what a people these are. I do not think one man among them could read a sermon without spelling a good part of it; and how would that edify the rest? Nor has any of our family a voice strong enough to be heard by such a number of people.

This letter was followed by another, equally as famous:

> Our meeting has wonderfully conciliated the minds of the people toward us, so that we now live in the greatest amity imaginable. Some families who seldom went to church, now go constantly; and one person who had not been there for seven years, is now prevailed to go with the rest.

Susanna's final paragraph demonstrates the brilliance of her mind and her diplomacy:

> If you do, after all, think fit to dissolve this

assembly, do not tell me that you *desire* me to do it,
for that will not satisfy my conscience; but send me
your *positive command*, in such full and express terms
as may absolve me from all guilt and punishment,
for neglecting this opportunity of doing good, when
you and I shall appear before the great and awful
tribunal of *Our Lord Jesus Christ*.

Since Samuel did not issue such a command,
Susanna continued to meet with this group which she
named *Our Society*.

Samuel Wesley purchased a new Polyglott Bible
together with other expensive reference sets. "The
world will remember me as the author of *The Dissertations on the Book of Job*," he assured Susanna.

Alone in his study, Samuel wrote the book in Latin;
using quotations in Greek, Hebrew, and other
languages. He also recorded variations of the text in
other languages. He searched the church fathers and
many ancient books hoping to find additional light
on Job.

Whenever there was a shortage of money, Samuel
would shake his head and say, "That's all right. Job
will supply our needs!"

As Samuel labored on Job, Susanna taught the
children. Her dream of producing children who would
help change the world still continued. To enable her
to do this, she produced a set of rules. Here they are
as she later outlined them to her son John.

1. It had been observed that cowardice and
fear of punishment often lead children into lying.
To prevent this a law was made that whoever
was charged with a fault of which they were
guilty, if they would . . . confess it and promise
to amend (they) should not be beaten.

2. That no sinful action, as lying, pilfering
at church or on the Lord's day, disobedience,

quarrelling, etc. should ever pass unpunished.

3. That no child should ever be chided or beat twice for the same fault, and that if they amended they should never be upraided with it afterwards.

4. That every signal act of obedience, especially when it crossed upon their own inclinations, should always be commended, and frequently rewarded according to the merits of the case.

5. That if ever any child performed an act of obedience, or did anything with an intention to please, though the performance was not well, yet the obedience and intention should be kindly accepted, and the child with sweetness directed how to do better for the future.

6. That propriety (the rights of property) be . . . preserved, and none suffered to invade the property of another in the smallest manner, though it were but the value of a farthing or a pin, which they might not take from the owner without, much less against, his consent.

7. That promises be strictly observed; and a gift once bestowed, and so the right passed away from the donor, be not resumed, but left to the disposal of him to who it was given, unless it were conditional, and the condition of the obligation not performed.

8. That no girl be taught to work till she can read very well.

At the end of a frustrating teaching session in 1714, Samuel burst into the room. He was pale and almost beside himself.

"What's the matter?" asked Susanna, putting her arm around him.

"We've come to the end of an era!"

"What do you mean?"

"Queen Anne is dead! And since none of her seventeen children are alive, the House of Stuart is no more."

"And who is the new king?"

"George I of the House of Hanover. He can't speak English, but he's the heir."

"How?"

"He's the great grandson of James I. The bloodline goes through Elizabeth, sister of Charles I."

From then on, the Church of England prayed for the king, the new Defender of the Faith and head of the Church of England. Soon the Wesleys returned to normal living.

One year as fall approached, Susanna had a gleam in her eye. She had seen a bolt of cloth at the store that would make a new dress for each of the girls and one for herself. She was about to mention the matter when Samuel said, "I'm afraid I'll have to buy some new books to help me complete Job."

Choking back her desire, Susanna said, "Job comes first! I want it to be a masterpiece." Samuel poured his time and money into this project. He hired helpers whom he could not afford and he had pictures drawn for the book when he lacked money for coal. But Susanna remained loyal. She wrote "Old as I am, since I have taken my husband for 'better, for worse,' I'll take my residence with him. Where he lives, will I live; and where he dies, will I die; and there I will be buried."

By 1724 Samuel was so deep in debt Susanna feared he would again be sent to prison. Every unexpected knock at the door sent chills down her spine. Then after opening a letter from the bishop, Samuel rushed to her side. Waving the letter, he exclaimed, "The Lord has helped us! With a little care we'll be rich. Did you hear that, Sukey? We'll be rich!"

Susanna frowned. "Rich?" she glanced at him sideways.

"Yes, we've been given the living at Wroot—and it pays 50 pounds a year. Since Wroot is only four and a half miles away I can handle both parishes." He paced around a bit and his enthusiasm grew. "There's a rectory at Wroot. That means we can move into it and rent this one. Oh, Sukey, the good Lord remembers his children."

"But that house is an old one. It's full of rats. It needs repairs. The roof leaks. It's surrounded by swamps. Sir, I think you'd better pray about it."

"I've already prayed about it. We'll be moving next week!"

Unconsciously Susanna stared. Then by force of habit she murmured, "Yes, master."

The congregation at Wroot was even more primitive than the one at Epworth. But those rustic people believed in eating, and they believed that the pastor and his family should also eat. Writing to John about the situation, Emilia noted, "We have plenty of good meat and drink (and) fuel, etc."

Financially, however, the Wesleys were just as burdened as they had been before the move. This was because Samuel had to hire an assistant. The only advantage was the rent from Epworth. And among the disadvantages was the fact that the roads between Epworth and Wroot were often so drenched with mud, transportation over them was all but impossible. At such times the Wesleys were forced to go by boat in a roundabout way through rivers and canals, and boat fares were expensive.

Susanna's health during these dark days was not good. Sometimes she was in bed for weeks. Just after their move to Wroot, she was inspired by a distant thread of hope. Word had come that her brother,

Samuel Annesley, was returning from India. She was confident that he was going to give her 1000 pounds!

Learning when the East India Company ship would dock in London, Susanna made arrangements to meet it. This was the first time that she had returned to London since she left.

She and her son Samuel had agreed that after the boat landed she would take her brother to his home in Westminster for a grand celebration. Alas, Samuel was not on the ship; nor was he ever heard from after this. From what little information they found, they could only assume that he had been murdered and his fortune stolen.

Following this disappointment, Susanna's husband had a slight stroke which disabled his right hand. But, as cheerful as ever, he wrote to his friend, Mr.Piggot, the vicar of nearby Doncaster, "I thank God, and I begin to put my left hand to school to learn to write, so that it can help its lame brother."

Susanna's sons, John, Charles, and Samuel, (even though away at school) were her great source of encouragement. All of them were physically short-sighted, scholarly, and, eventually, deeply spiritual. Three years later, Samuel became a King's Scholar, and this provided financial assistance to continue at Westminister. Later, he enrolled at Christ Church at Oxford. Here, he earned his M.A. degree. Later, he was ordained a priest in the Church of England. But preferring educational work to preaching, he spent the rest of his life teaching at Westminster.

Charles and John were also excellent scholars. Like Samuel, Charles did his preliminary work at Westminster and then continued at Christ Church. John started out at Charterhouse. Then, like his brothers, earned his degree at Christ Church. In addition, he was elected a Fellow of Lincoln. This

fellowship allowed him to continue his studies at
Oxford, and permitted him to do private teaching to
earn extra money. It also provided him with a suite
of rooms—rent free. Moreover, it was his privilege
to rent these rooms to others during his absence, and
to keep the rent. And this he did for twenty-six years.

Samuel, Susanna's husband, was so excited by
John's success, he exclaimed, "Whatever I am, my
Jack is a fellow of Lincoln!"

While John and Charles were attending Oxford,
the morals of the students were extremely low. Drinking, gambling, idleness, and loose living were common. Both John and Charles rebelled at this. Charles
wrote: "Diligence led me into serious thinking. I went
to the weekly sacrament, and persuaded two or three
young students to accompany me, and to observe the
method of study prescribed by the statutes of the
University. This gave me the harmless name of
Methodist."

Soon, this little group increased until it had as many
as twenty-five members. From Susanna, Charles had
learned the value of method; and, now that he had
founded this group which was soon to be known as
the Holy Club, methods became part of their system.
Each minute of day had its purpose. There was a certain time for prayer, fasting, studying the Bible,
distributing alms, visiting prisoners, group discus-
sions, taking communion, and so on.

It was because of these methods, members of the
Holy Club were sneered at as being Methodists. And
it was because Charles Wesley had founded the Holy
Club that he is revered as being the *first* Methodist.

While John and Charles continued at Oxford,
Susanna kept up a steady correspondence with them.
She encouraged them, discussed fine points in
theology, and gave advice. She rejoiced when they

were ordained priests in the Church of England. But she refused to insist that they follow this course. That task, she felt, was the work of the Holy Spirit.

George I died in 1727 and was immediately followed to the throne by his son, George II, who had also been born in Hanover. At the time, Samuel made a wry comment: "I have now dedicated books to two queens, Mary II and Anne. This means that Job will be dedicated to the new one, Queen Caroline!"

More than ever, Job became the center of Samuel's life. Taking notes and writing with his left hand was extremely difficult. Soon he employed John Romley to take dictation and help with research. "Time is short and I must work while it is day," he explained to Susanna.

Sometimes it seemed to Samuel that he was trying to tunnel through a mountain with a broken spoon. But when the impossibilities seemed greatest, a ray of light always appeared. In 1730, a copy of a letter written by Alexander Pope to Dean Swift, came to his attention. After reading it in one ecstatic gulp, he shouted for Susanna to come to his study. "Listen to this," he admonished, holding the letter in his left hand. "And as I read it, remember it is from one of the world's greatest writers to another of the world's greatest writers!" Eyes sparkling, he read:

> This is a letter extraordinary, to do and say nothing but to recommend to you a pious and good work, and for a good and honest man; moreover, he is about seventy and poor. I shall think it a kindness done to myself, if you can propagate Mr. Wesley's subject for his Commentary on Job among your divines (bishops excepted, of whom there is no hope,) and among such as are believers, or readers of Scripture. Lord Bolingbroke is a favorer of it, and it allows you to do your best to serve an old Tory, though you are a Whig, as I am.

"Oh, I'm so proud of you," said Susanna. "And, sir, I'm convinced that it will be a great book. Someday, it will be on the same shelf with *Paradise Lost* and *Gulliver's Travels!*"

"That letter, Sukey, will get me many subscriptions. But," he sighed and massaged his paralyzed right hand, "you must pray for me. I'm as weary as Moses was when they had to hold up his hands."

"Don't worry, sir, I pray for you every day."

On another occasion when his gloom was at a dark point, Samuel saw a list of his subscriptions. After marking the most distinguished names, he summoned Susanna. "Some men of quality are buying Job," he said. He then read the list. It included fifteen bishops and twenty-two deans. "And besides these, thirty-one nobles are subscribing," he added.

On June 4, 1731, Samuel was almost killed. Susanna described the accident in a letter to John. "I, your sister Martha, and our maid, were going in a wagon to see the ground we hire of Mrs. Knight. Samuel sat in a chair at one end of the wagon, I in another at the other end, Matty between us, and the maid behind me. Just before we reached the close, the horses took into a gallop; and out flew your father and his chair. The maid seeing the horses run, hung all her weight on my chair, and kept me from keeping him company. She cried out to Williams to stop the horses, that her master was killed. The fellow leaped out of the seat, stayed the horses, then ran to Mr. Wesley, but, ere he got to him, two neighbors, who were providentially met together, raised his head, upon which he had been pitched, and held him backward, by which means he began to respire; for it is certain by the blackness of his face, that he had never drawn breath from the time of his fall until they helped him up.

"I informed him (Samuel) of his fall. He said he 'knew nothing of any fall.' "

The nearly dead man was taken home and bled. And, although he continued to claim that he had not been hurt, he slowly worsened. His heart remained with Job. "I-I must f-finish it," he muttered again and again. "That book will pay my debts, buy clothes for Sukey and the girls. It will furnish the rectory."

"Yes, and it will give you the fame you deserve," added Susanna.

John, Charles, and Samuel visited him whenever they could and helped with the project. John spent an entire summer with him, preaching at both Wroot and Epworth. The manuscript on Job continued to thicken.

By 1735 the Wesleys had been in Epworth for thirty-nine years. Still, little progress had been made. Drunks continued to stagger on the streets. Many continued to swear. Gambling was still popular. The attendance at St. Andrews was sparse. Illiteracy remained high. But Epworth had become a part of Susanna and Samuel's very being. Twelve of their children had been born here. And five of them had died and were buried here. They loved the little town.

Samuel became so feeble there were times he had to be helped into the pulpit. His face had became so thin his wig was far too large. To some, it made him look grotesque. He was often discouraged. But his discouragement never lasted more than a few minutes.

When alone with Susanna, he would hold her tight with his left arm and murmur, "Remember, Sukey, God's Word is true—every word of it! And remember the Good Book says, 'Cast thy bread upon the waters: for thou shalt find it after many days,' (Eccl. 11:1). You and I have cast a lot of bread upon the waters, haven't we?"

"We surely have," replied Susanna each time, "and I believe there will be a harvest."

Samuel's accident had sapped his health, but so had the sorrow of the previous year. Many years before when a charity boy, Johnnie Whitelamb, was turned over to the Wesleys for board and training, Samuel had all but adopted him. He employed him as a secretary to work on Job, and eventually helped him to enroll at Oxford where he was enthusiastically tutored by John.

Eventually Johnnie was ordained and became the curate at Wroot. In 1733 he had asked for the hand of Molly, who was then thirty-seven. Samuel gave his consent even though Johnnie was several years younger than Molly. Alas, the next year both Molly and her infant son died. They were buried together in the Wroot churchyard on November 1, 1734. It was a heavy blow.

At the funeral, Susanna said, sobbing, "Molly was such a dear. I'll never forget those bright eyes! And her laughter was like tinkling bells."

Samuel held Susanna in his arms and tried to comfort her. "Molly was a special gift from the Lord," he said.

During the winter of 1735 Samuel was forced to abandon all work on his commentary. But as feeble as he became, his mind remained clear. Motioning John to his bedside, he said in a clear voice, "The inward witness, son, the inward witness, that is the strongest witness of Christianity."

On another occasion, Samuel summoned Charles. After placing his left hand on his son's head, he said, "Be steady. The Christian faith will surely revive in this kingdom; you shall see it, though I shall not."

Later, he signaled for Emily to bend her head close. While she listened, he whispered, "Do not be

concerned about my death. God will then begin to
manifest himself to my family.'' Just before he lost
his voice, someone asked, ''Are the consolations of
God small with you?''

In reply, Samuel answered, ''No, no, no.'' After
that, he named each one standing by his bed. Next,
he admonished them, ''Think of heaven, talk of
heaven; all the time is lost when we are not thinking
of heaven.''

As the weeks passed, Susanna stayed by his bedside. In a letter written to John she had said, '' 'Tis
an unhappiness almost peculiar to our family, that
your father and I seldom think alike.'' But she was
deeply in love with him and was utterly convinced of
his genius.

Susanna's strength was limited. During Samuel's
final weeks she fainted at least once and had to be carried out of his room. Indeed, at the time of his passing, she had been confined to her separate room for
several days.

The sun had just reddened the west when Samuel
died on April 25 at the age of seventy-two. He was
buried ''very frugally, yet decently, in the churchyard
according to his own desire.'' Both Charles and John
were at the funeral.

The day was marred by Mrs. Knight. Noticing that
she had rounded up the cattle belonging to his parents,
John approached her. ''Why are you driving away
the cattle?'' he asked.

''Because Sam Wesley owes me 15 pounds land
rent!'' she announced.

With effort, John persuaded her to accept his note
for the debt. This having been done, and his signature
witnessed, she returned to her carriage and drove off.

The children had feared that Susanna would be
unable to stand the strain. But she had lingered before

the Lord, had checked her compass, and understood
that God had a plan for her. In a way, she felt alone,
and yet she knew God was with her.

Alone

Widowhood was hard for Susanna. She missed Samuel's voice with his sudden announcements: ''I've learned something new about Job. Listen!'' And even his orders. Twice she was awakened by a dream in which she heard him say, ''The trouble, Sukey, is that people don't have enough faith. If only they would believe in the Word!''

At the time of his death, Sam owed approximately 100 pounds. And he didn't have a will. In the meantime, the widow of Susanna's brother Samuel had providentially provided her with the income from 1000 pounds for life.

While these shifts and arrangements were being made, John and Charles were uncomfortable. Both were concerned because they had agreed to do missionary work in Georgia where General James Oglethorpe had founded a colony. Neither would have gone had Susanna objected. But when they approached her at the opening of the opportunity, she had replied with unusual animation, ''Had I twenty sons, I should rejoice that they were so employed, though I should never see them more."

Emilia had opened a school in Gainsborough and Susanna moved in with her. This move pleased everyone; especially Susanna, for she remained a teacher at heart.

John and Charles were uneasy about "abandoning" their mother. Then one of them had an inspiration. "Let's finish Job and see it through the press!" Susanna was enthusiastic. Daniel Defoe, friend of her youth, had published *Robinson Crusoe* in 1719. And it had gone through countless printings and had done a lot of good. It was still selling all over the world— and in many languages. Perhaps the *Dissertations on Job* would also be a helpful book and become a monument to Samuel.

Job was duly finished and two days before John was scheduled to sail to America, he presented a copy to Queen Caroline, the one to whom it had been dedicated. Dressed in his finest, and briefed on protocol, John was formally presented to Her Majesty. When he entered the room, the young queen was romping with her maids of honor.

As instructed, John held out the book as he knelt on one knee. "It is very prettily bound," she said. Then, after some other comments, and without even opening it, she laid it down, returned to her friends, and continued her romping.

John was disappointed. He had hoped that she would have at least opened it. After all, the book represented twenty-five years of extremely hard work! But, according to protocol, his face remained expressionless as he slowly backed out of the room.

On October 14, 1735, John and Charles took a boat from Gravesend in order to embark for Georgia. That afternoon they boarded the *Simmonds*. Although their

mother was absent, her influence was still with them.
The idea of method which they had learned from her
had become part of the fiber of their lives. They had
agreed to be engaged in private prayer each morning from four till five; to study the Bible together from
five till seven; to breakfast from seven until eight; from
eight until nine to have public prayers; and to continue on in this manner until they retired for the night
between nine and ten. It was a hectic schedule.

During their third month at sea, the *Simmonds* was
caught in a terrible storm. John recorded the event
in his journal. "At noon our third storm began. At
four it was more violent than before. The winds roared
about us. The ship not only rocked . . . with the utmost
violence, but shook and jarred with so unequal,
grating motion, that one could not but with great difficulty keep one's hold of anything, nor stand a
moment without it. Every ten minutes came a shock
from the stern or side of the ship, which one would
think would dash the planks to pieces.

"At seven I went to the Germans (they were called
Moravians and were on their way to Georgia). I had
long before observed the great seriousness of their
behavior. Of their humility they had given me con-
tinual proof. And every day had given them occasion
of showing a meekness which no injury could remove.
If they were pushed, struck, or thrown down, they
rose again and went away; but no complaint was
found in their mouth. There was now an opportunity
of trying whether they were delivered from the spirit
of fear, as well as from that of pride, anger and
revenge. In the midst of the psalm wherewith their
service began, the sea broke over, split the main-sail
in pieces, covered the ship, and poured in between
the decks, as if the great deep had already swallowed
us up. A terrible screaming began among the English.

The Moravians calmly sung on. I asked one of them afterwards, '(Were) you not afraid?' He answered, 'I thank God, no.' I asked, 'But were not your women and children afraid?'' He replied, mildly, 'No; our women and children are not afraid to die.''

The storm stopped at noon. But the turmoil in Wesley's heart did not stop. Again and again he questioned himself, ''What is it that these Moravian brethren have that I do not have?'' *Could it be*, he wondered, *that there is more to Christianity than the mere reading of prayers and the quoting of Scripture?*

While John and Charles tossed on the Atlantic, Susanna faced another disappointment. Only 500 copies of Job had been printed, and less than 400 copies had been sold. It was a financial disaster. Moreover, some of the comments about the book had been caustic. In a letter to Bishop Hurd, Bishop Warburton had said, ''Poor Job! It was his eternal fate to be persecuted by his friends. His three comforters passed sentences of condemnation upon him, and he has been (executed in effigy) ever since.'' He then accused Wesley of having ''cut'' him up.

Susanna's dreams were like shredded paper. They had not come to pass. Of her nineteen children, ten were already dead. True, her three sons had master's degrees from Oxford; but most of the girls had been disappointments. Several of their marriages had been difficult; and, although all of them were educationally advanced beyond most women, none had sought higher education.

After almost four months on the ocean, the *Simmonds* reached the Savannah river on February 5, 1736. Both John and Charles were utterly wearied by their trip. Still, both remained intrigued by the Christ-like lives of the Moravians.

Approaching Mr. Spangenberg, one of the

Moravian pastors, John questioned him about the
serenity of his people. In reply, the pastor said, "My
brother, I must first ask you one or two questions.
Have you the witness within yourself? Does the Spirit
of God bear witness with your spirit that you are a
child of God?" Numbed by the question, John
remained silent.

Then Spangenberg had another question. "Do you
know Jesus Christ?"

"I know that he is the Saviour of the world," replied
John after a pause.

"True," replied the German. "But do you know
that he has saved *you*?"

The pastor's emphasis on *you* startled John. Didn't
the man know that he had an Oxford degree, that he
was a Fellow of Lincoln College, an ordained priest,
the son of an ordained priest, an ardent student of
the Bible, a missionary, and that he had served as a
curate? And didn't he know that he had been baptized as an infant, that he had been raised in the
church, and that his parents were godly people?

Finally, John Wesley gulped, "I hope . . . He
. . . died to save me." But his words had a doubtful
ring in them.

Neither John nor Charles was happy in Georgia.
After numerous misunderstandings with the gover-
nor, Charles left for England on July 26. He had been
in Georgia slightly more than five months. John
remained. But he, too, was uncomfortable; and after
a few days over twenty-two months, he left for
England on December 22, 1737. In his own opinion
his stay had been a complete failure. But this was not
entirely true, for he had published America's first
hymnal and organized America's first Sunday school.

As Susanna visited with her weary sons, she was
disappointed. Neither overflowed with glowing tales

of success. And since Charles was nearly thirty and John thirty-four, more than half their lives were apparently gone. Likewise, her feelings of uselessness skidded to new lows because neither of her boys was well received in England. Again and again her sense of frustration was so keen she felt sick in the pit of her stomach. *Could it be that her motherly ambition had deflected her compass?*

Neither John nor Charles had been converted to the Moravian faith. But each had been definitely influenced. Moreover, Peter Böhler, another Moravian, had kept in contact with them in London. Realizing that he should preach faith, John was puzzled; for he, himself, had very little faith. Approaching Peter, he asked, "But what can I preach?"

Peter replied: "Preach faith *till* you have it; and then because you have it, you *will* preach faith."

John followed his friend's advice. But this led to problems, as indicated by his Journal.

Tues. 9. I preached at Great St. Helen's. . .on "He spared not his own Son, but delivered Him up for us all." My heart was now so enlarged to declare the love of God to all that were oppressed by the devil, that I did not wonder in the least when I was afterward told, "Sir, you must preach here no more."

Sun. 14. I preached in the morning at St. Ann's, Aldersgate; and in the afternoon at the Savoy chapel, free salvation in the blood of Christ. I was quickly apprized that at St. Ann's, likewise, I am to preach no more.

And so it went. The pulpit was closed to him at St. John's, Wapping, at St. Bennett's, at Paul's-Warf, and other places. Charles, too, was ignored.

With almost every door bolted in front of them, Charles and John (and Susanna with them) were dismayed and heartbroken. Neither Charles nor John knew that an amazing breakthrough which would transform England was less than two weeks away.

Kezzy had a breakthrough experience in which she realized that Christ had come to earth to die for her sins. Her feeling of assurance was so profound and so visible that Charles was inspired to write one of his greatest hymns:

> Love divine, all love excelling
>   Joy of Heaven, to earth come down,
> Fix in us Thy humble dwelling
>   All thy faithful mercies crown.

Following Kezzy's "conversion," Charles had his own encounter with the Lord. His was in a row-house—number 12—in Little Britain, a short street that right-angles from Aldersgate. His conversion was on May 21, and was the result of a "poor ignorant mechanic who knew nothing but Christ."

Three days later, feeling that he had never really been converted, John Wesley concentrated on studying the New Testament. To his amazement, he learned that the conversion experience was almost always an instantaneous one. Troubled, he continued to consult with Böhler, and then with Böhler's friends. Finally convinced that simple faith was the answer, he resolved in his own words to renounce "all dependence in whole or in part, upon my *own works* or righteousness."

But pray as he would, nothing *seemed* to happen.

Then at about five in the morning on Wesnesday, May 24, 1738, he opened his Greek New Testament to 2 Peter 1:4. There, he read: "Whereby are given unto us exceedingly great and precious promises; that by these ye might be partakers of the divine nature." Afterward, just as he left the house, he read the words of Jesus: "Thou art not far from the kingdom of God" (Mark 12:34). In the afternoon he was invited by a friend to attend a service in the nearby St. Paul's Cathedral.

Curiously, the anthem was Psalm 130. Backgrounded by music of Henry Purcell, former organist of Westminster Abbey, the words were: "Out of the deep have I called unto Thee, O Lord; Lord, hear my voice."

John listened intently, for that anthem fitted his need as closely as a glove fits a hand. What happened after that? Turning to his journal we read: "In the evening I went very unwillingly to a society in Aldersgate-Street, where one was reading Luther's preface to the Epistle to the Romans. About a quarter till nine, while he was describing the change which God works in the heart through faith in Christ, I felt my heart strangely warmed, I felt that I did trust in Christ, Christ alone for salvation: and an assurance was given me, that he had taken away *my* sins, even *mine*, and saved *me* from the law of sin and death."

Assured of personal salvation through Christ, John and Charles began to have a crowded ministry. Soon, both were preaching many times each day. And when the churches were bolted against them, they preached in the streets, in the fields, at public gatherings. At first, they attacted a few, then hundreds, then thousands, then tens of thousands. George Whitefield suggested field preaching. John was horrified. Then he remembered how his mother had led services in the kitchen, and how transforming those services had been. Thus encouraged, he took the plunge and was soon observing gutters in the coal miners' faces as their tears washed away the dust.

They preached in the streets, in the fields, at public

gatherings. At first, they attracted a few, then hundreds, then thousands, then tens of thousands.

John preached and organized societies. Charles preached and wrote hymns. And soon all of England was singing such personal reflections of divine grace as *O For a Thousand Tongues to Sing*, and *Come O Thou Traveller Unknown*.

A spiritual fire, far more vigorous than the London fire of 1666 had been lit. But this fire, ignited in Little Britain and Aldersgate, did not reach its maximum at Pie Corner—and then go out. No, it leaped oceans, and within a few years encircled the world.

But there were doubters. And these doubters included Samuel, Jr.—and Susanna! As she listened and watched, she wondered if the message preached by John and Charles was of the Lord. Could it be that her sons had become mentally unbalanced due to their trip to Georgia?

Susanna, however was not the only one with doubts. Raised on the belief that no one could be absolutely certain of salvation, and that good works are necessary for salvation, John and Charles were often inclined to be cautious, especially in their lonely hours.

John and Charles' study of the converts, however, convinced them. Drunkards were sobered; wife-beaters became loving; thieves returned stolen goods. Moreover, each convert was convinced of his salvation—instant though it was.

While Susanna's heart remained shaded with doubt, she went to stay with Martha—nicknamed Patty. Martha had married a Church of England clergyman named Hall.

While participating in a communion service, as her son-in-law handed her the cup, his words, ''The blood of our Lord Jesus Christ which was given for thee,'' suddenly came to life in her heart. Relating the occasion afterwards she wrote, ''The words struck through my heart, and I knew that God, for Christ's sake, had forgiven me all my sins.''

And thus, Susanna Wesley had her evangelical conversion. At the time, she was a little over seventy!

A short time after this, Samuel, Jr., died at the age of forty-nine. Since he was her first and oldest child, this was a double blow. His death meant that only eight of her nineteen children remained alive.

Neither John or Charles wished to start a new denomination. To them, the Church of England was the finest denomination ever conceived. Their whole objective was to cultivate societies that would help put new life in the Church of England. And because of this, they attended the Church of England on Sunday, and urged their followers to do the same.

But as societies increased in number and size,

buildings were needed. In the fall of 1739 John Wesley took over an old foundry in London that had been ruined by an explosion. This building was converted into a place of worship, and a building connected with it turned into a dwelling place. Eventually Susanna moved into this home. She was close to her children.

The flame of the new movement continued to spread. It was as if an eighteenth century Pentecost had taken place. John and Charles kept their horses busy riding from one appointment to the next. But all was not peaceful. There were riots, and both brothers were threatened with imprisonment. But the more the *Methodists* were persecuted, the faster they expanded. Indeed, many in positions of authority were converted.

Kezziah died less than three years after Samuel, Jr.'s, death. Now Susanna had only seven surviving children.

During her sorrows, she had moments of doubts concerning her conversion. But like the doubts that assailed John and Charles, they were soon replaced by the ''inward witness'' extolled by her husband on his deathbed.

On June 5, 1742, John rode into Epworth, checked into the Red Lion Hotel, and the next morning walked over to St. Andrew's. Since he had been raised in this parish, and had frequently preached in its pulpit, he fully expected the pastor either to invite him to preach; or, at least, to take part in the service.

But Mr. Romley, the curate, didn't see it that way. This was a surprise to John since he and Romley had been old friends, and Romley had been a curate under his father. Nonetheless, John slipped into a pew and enjoyed the morning service.

At the afternoon service, the building was crowded; for rumor had spread that John Wesley was going to preach. Instead, John was ignored and Romley preached a biting sermon against enthusiasm. The sermon was obviously directed at John Wesley.

After the service, John Taylor took a position in the churchyard and calmly announced that John Wesley would preach outside in the yard at six o'clock.

That evening the yard was black with the largest throng John Wesley had ever seen at Epworth. Among the people stood his former student and brother-in-law, Johnnie Whitelamb, the curate at Wroot. Positioning himself on his father's tomb, John preached on the text: "The kingdom of heaven is not meat and drink; but righteousness, and peace, and joy in the Holy Ghost" (Romans 14:17).

As he preached, a stillness settled over the people. Some began to wipe their eyes and others to nod their heads. At the conclusion, he was invited to speak in many surrounding villages. And at each village, Burnham, Haxey, Ouston, Belton, and others, he met with large crowds. In each place cheeks were dampened. As in London, the natives of Lincolnshire were thirsty for the Gospel.

The fact that sinners could be saved was indeed Good News.

When Susanna learned about the revival that had broken out at Epworth and its satellite villages she was ecstatically happy. "When your father was dying, "he put his hand on Charles' head and said, 'Be steady. The Christian faith will surely revive in this kingdom; you shall see it, though I shall not."

"I guess Father was a prophet," said John.

"He certainly was," agreed Susanna.

Late in July, 1742, John learned while he was in Bristol that his mother was seriously ill. After riding to London on horseback he immediately went to the

Foundry. His Journal for July 23 records what happened:

> About three in the afternoon I went to my mother, and her change was near. I sat down on the bedside. She was in her last conflict; unable to speak, but I believe quite sensible. Her look was calm and serene, and her eyes fixed upward, while we commended her soul to God. From three to four the silver chord was loosing, and the wheel breaking at the cistern; and then without a struggle, or sigh, or groan, the soul was set at liberty. We stood around the bed and fulfilled her last request, uttered a little before she lost her speech.

That final request was: "Children, as soon as I am released, sing a psalm of praise to God." Assured that she was gone, John, Patty, Nancy, Emilia, Hetty, and Sukey, joined together in singing a psalm that their mother especially loved. At the time, all of her living children with the exception of Charles, were present. All were believers.

Funeral services were conducted by John. Again, his journal tells the story:

> *Sunday*, August 1. Almost an innumerable company of people being gathered together, about five in the afternoon I committed to the earth the body of my mother.

Susanna was buried in Bunhill Fields—the Westminister Abbey of Dissenters. This was an appropriate place; for near her grave are those of her sister Elizabeth, Isaac Watts, Daniel Defoe, John Bunyan, and a host of others who gave their lives for the Word.

The influence of Susanna continued to burn within the hearts of her sons. Charles wrote hymns until he was past 80. John continued his ministry into his 87th year. Four days before his passing, John addressed his final letter to William Wilberforce, the near-hunchback who was fighting slavery in the House of Commons. That flaming letter included the lines, "O 'be not weary in well doing!' Go on, in the name of God and in the power of His might, till even American slavery (the vilest that ever saw the sun) shall vanish before it."

Had Susanna read that letter, she would have said, "Amen!" She would have rejoiced in knowing that the tiny flame she and Samuel had lit was still burning.

SUSANNA WESLEY'S CHILDREN*

	Name	Birthplace	Born	Died	Age
1.	Samuel, Jr.	London	2/10/1690	11/6/1739	49
2.	Susanna	South Ormsby	1691	4/1693	Infant
3.	Emilia	"	1/1692	1771	79
4.	Annesley	twins "	1694	1/31/1695	Infants
5.	Jedediah				
6.	Susanna (Sukey)	"	1695	12/7/1764	69
7.	Mary (Molly)	"	1696	11/1734	38
8.	Mehetabel (Hetty)	Epworth	1697	3/21/1750	53
9.	Sex Unknown	"	1698	?	Infant
10.	John	"	5/18/1699	?	Infant
11.	Benjamin	"	1700	?	Infant
12.	Unnamed	twins "	5/17/1701	?	Infants
13.	Unnamed				
14.	Anne (Nancy)	"	1702	?	Infant
15.	John Benjamin (Jackie)	"	6/17/1703	3/2/1791	87
16.	Unnamed	"	5/8/1705	5/30/1705	Infant
17.	Martha (Patty)	"	5/8/1706	7/19/1791	85
18.	Charles	"	12/18/1707	3/29/1788	80
19.	Kezziah (Kezzy)	"	3/9/1709	3/9/1742	32

* Major help for this chart was received from the book *Susanna, Mother of the Wesleys* by Rebecca Lamar Harmon, published by Abingdon Press. Copyright 1968.

IMPORTANT EVENTS IN HISTORY

1509—1547   Henry VIII
1519   Luther openly denied power of Pope
1534   Henry VIII made head of Church of England
1547—1553   Edward VI
1553—1558   Mary Tudor
1558—1603   Elizabeth I

1603—1625   James I
1611   Publication of Authorized (King James' Version) of the Bible
1620   Birth of Dr. Samuel Annesley
1625—1649   Charles I
1642—1648   Civil War
1649   Charles I beheaded
1649   Commonwealth established under Cromwell

1653—1658   One-man rule under Oliver Cromwell
1658—1660   Richard Cromwell
1660—1685   Charles II (Restoration of monarchy)
1662   Act of Uniformity
1662   Birth of Samuel Wesley
1666   Great Fire of London
1669   Birth of Susanna Annesley

1685—1688   James II

1685	Edict of Nantes cancelled by Louis XIV
1689?	Samuel Wesley married to Susanna Annesley
1689—1694	William III and Mary
1694—1702	William III
1697	The Wesleys move to Epworth
1702—1714	Anne (Last of the Stuarts)
1703	Birth of John Benjamin Wesley
1707	Birth of Charles Wesley
1714—1727	George I (First of the House of Hanover)
1727—1760	George II
1735	Death of Samuel Wesley
1742	Death of Susanna Wesley

BIBLIOGRAPHY

Those desiring to learn more about Susanna Wesley and this period will find the following books especially useful.

Albright, Raymond W. *The History of the Protestant Episcopal Church*. Macmillan, 1964.

Besant, Sir Walter. *London in the Eighteenth Century*. London, 1925.

Besant, Sir Walter. *London in the Time of the Stuarts*. London, 1903.

Burton, Elizabeth. *The Pageant of Georgian England*. Scribners, 1967.

Cameron, Richard M. *The Rise of Methodism*. Philosophical Library, 1954.

Churchill, Sir Winston. *A History of the English Speaking Peoples*, Vol. III. Dodd and Mead, 1964.

Clarke, Adam. *Memoirs of the Wesley Family*. Lane and Tppett, 1848.

Clarke, Eliza. *Susanna Wesley*. W.H. Allen, London, 1886.

Curnock, Nehemiah. *The Journal of John Wesley*. Vol. 1-8. Epworth Press, 1938.

Defoe, Daniel. *A Journal of the Plague Year*. Heritage Press, 1968.

Durant, Will and Ariel. *The Age of Louis XIV*. Simon and Schuster, 1963.

Earle, Peter. *The World of Daniel Defoe*. Weidenfeld and Nicolscn, 1976.

Fraser, Antonia. *Royal Charles*. Knopf, 1979.

Fraser, Antonia. *Cromwell, the Lord Protector*. Knopf, 1979.

Fraser, Antonia. *Mary Queen of Scots*. Delacarte, 1978.

Gill, Frederick C. *Charles Wesley, the First Methodist.*
Abingdon, 1964.

Green, David. *Queen Anne.* Collins, 1970.

Hale, Robert. *Sir Christopher Wren.* Bryan Little,
1975.

Harmon, Rebecca Lamar. *Susanna — Mother of the
Wesleys.* Abingdon, 1968.

Kirk, John. *The Mother of the Wesleys.* Poe and
Hitchcok, 1867.

Martyn, Carlos. *Life and Times of Milton.* Norwood
Editions, 1977.

Newton, John A. *Susanna Wesley.* Epworth Press, 1968.

Ogg, David. *England in the Reign of Charles II.* Oxford,
1934.

Payne, Robert. *The Christian Centuries.* W.W. Norton,
1966.

Tyreman, Luke. *The Life and Times of Samuel Wesley.*
Simpkin and Marshall & Co. 1866.

Wakely, J.B. *Heroes of Methodism.* Carlton Porter,
1856.

Winslow, Ola Elizabeth. *John Bunyan.* Macmillan,
1961.

INDEX

SOWERS SERIES

ATHLETE
Billy Sunday, Home Run to Heaven
by Robert Allen

EXPLORERS AND PIONEERS
Christopher Columbus, Adventurer of Faith and Courage
by Bennie Rhodes
Johnny Appleseed, God's Faithful Planter, John Chapman
by David Collins

HOMEMAKERS
Abigail Adams, First Lady of Faith and Courage
by Evelyn Witter
Susanna Wesley, Mother of John and Charles
by Charles Ludwig

HUMANITARIANS
Florence Nightingale, God's Servant at the Battlefield
by David Collins
Teresa of Calcutta, Serving the Poorest of the Poor
by D. Jeanene Watson

MUSICIANS AND POETS
Francis Scott Key, God's Courageous Composer
by David Collins
Samuel Francis Smith, My Country, 'Tis of Thee
by Marguerite E. Fitch